Great Flying Adventures

True accounts of eleven spine-tingling aviation exploits.

Great Flying Adventures

by Sherwood Harris

Illustrated with photographs

Random House New York

Copyright © 1973 by Sherwood Harris. All rights reserved under International and Pan-American Copyright Conventions. Published in the United States by Random House, Inc., New York, and simultaneously in Canada by Random House of Canada Limited, Toronto. Manufactured in the United States of America

Library of Congress Cataloging in Publication Data
Harris, Sherwood.   Great flying adventures.
SUMMARY: Details the aeronautical exploits of eleven men and women.
1. Aeronautics—Juvenile literature.   [1.   Aeronautics]   I.   Title.
TL547.H23   629.13′099910′.4   73–4243
ISBN 0-394-82438-5   ISBN 0-394-82438-1 (lib. bdg.)

Contents

Great Flying Adventures

Introduction

In flying, the unexpected can always happen.

One quiet Sunday morning in December 1965, two young men in a small, single-engined Aeronca Champion took off from a New Jersey airfield and headed down the Hudson River for New York City. The pilot, 19-year-old Philip Ippolito, had just gotten his private pilot's license a few months before and was on his way to do some sightseeing over the city.

It was a lovely day, cold but clear, and there were few other planes to bother Ippolito and his friend. They flew down the river for a while, then climbed up over New York to enjoy the view. The tall buildings of Manhattan rose like a giant piece of

Philip Ippolito's plane on the George Washington Bridge after his daring landing attempt.

modern steel-and-glass sculpture, and the sunlight flashed from millions of windows in jeweled hues of red, orange, and yellow.

Suddenly the engine began to sputter.

Here was a pilot's nightmare come true. There is no place to make an emergency landing in midtown New York without crashing among the towering buildings and steep, canyonlike streets. The men were within gliding distance of the ice-filled Hudson River. There was a slim chance they could land in the water and be rescued before they froze to death.

"Can you swim?" Ippolito shouted to his passenger.

"Not a stroke!" said his friend. Now even that slim chance was gone.

Ippolito remembered that automobile traffic had been unusually light when they had flown over the immense George Washington Bridge, which crosses the Hudson several miles north of New York's business district. In desperation he turned back toward the bridge, hoping to find a stretch of the broad roadway clear enough of cars for him to land. As he passed over the bridge, his engine quit completely and the little plane became a glider. Ippolito nosed over to maintain his flying speed and turned until he was lined up with the roadway. His plane sank lower and lower between two rows of huge cables on which the roadway was suspended. It rocked and bucked in the gusts of a 20-mile-per-hour crosswind.

Ippolito lined up on the center lane, praying that no cars would get in his way. He banked wildly to stop the crosswind from drifting him into the frightening web of cables on either side, leveled his wings at the last moment, and touched down. The landing would have been perfect, but his wingtip was grazed by a fast-moving trailer truck just as he landed, and the little plane was spun around and damaged before it finally came to rest. Philip Ippolito and his friend walked away from the landing with only minor cuts and bruises.

Over the years, as you will see in this book, airplanes in trouble have landed in some pretty strange places—on mountain slopes, in farmers' fields, in the open ocean, on the Arctic ice—but never before had a plane landed on a suspension bridge. Philip Ippolito's piloting skill in letting down in a crosswind between the two rows of cables was absolutely incredible. But it also took a lot of nerve to attempt such a daring landing. And it took a cool hand on the controls to keep the unexpected engine failure from turning into a disaster.

In the true stories that follow, you will meet more pilots whose skill, nerve, and cool reactions to unexpected situations led to some of the greatest adventures in the colorful history of flying. Some of the pilots in these stories were pioneers in the early days of aviation. Others flew in planes that can be seen today at any large airport. Many of these men and women achieved great fame in their flying careers.

But there are some, like Philip Ippolito, who are not well known. Until this book was written, their stories were told mainly when flying people got together to talk shop.

Only 70 years have passed since the Wright brothers made the world's first airplane flight at Kitty Hawk, North Carolina. In many ways, that flight, which lasted only a few seconds, was the greatest flying adventure of them all, for it made a dream of centuries come true, and it changed the world forever. But that flight did something more— it opened the skies to a new breed of men and women whose exploits are almost beyond belief to those of us with our feet still on the ground.

On the Plateau of the Three Condors

At 13,775 feet the plane has reached its limit. The engine barely has enough power to keep the plane that high, even at full throttle. Every time the pilot starts a turn he feels a shudder, warning him that his wings are about to lose their lift. He eases forward on his controls to keep from stalling, picks up a little bit of speed, and begins a gentle turn. He completes a half circle, then nurses the plane back up to its limit until he feels the warning buffeting of a stall again.

Behind the plane to the west, the verdant plains of Chile, jeweled with lakes and rivers, stretch down to the deep blue of the Pacific Ocean. Ahead tower the somber, snow-capped peaks of the Andes. The pilot can see sharp granite summits thrusting up above 20,000 feet and a maze of dead-end canyons with sheer walls and boulder-strewn floors. "I'm finished if I ever get trapped in one of those," he thinks.

He continues his wide, slow circles, fighting for every inch of altitude. "There must be a way through," the pilot keeps repeating to himself as he looks for an opening in the forbidding barrier. Today, of course, modern jets fly high enough to cross the Andes with room to spare. But in 1929, as French pilot Jean Mermoz attempts to establish an air mail route from Chile to Argentina, he must find a pass low enough for the planes of his day to slip through easily.

He spots a pass whose entrance lies about 1,000 feet above him. As he circles before it, he feels his plane rise on a strong upward-flowing current of air. The needle on his altimeter moves toward 15,000 feet, then stops. The plane begins to sink again.

Of all the pilots in the French air mail service, Mermoz has spent more time exploring the Andes than anyone else. He knows that eastward-flowing air currents off the Pacific tend to rise as they meet the mountains, so he circles patiently until he feels his plane lift again. Still not enough. A third updraft billows beneath his wings, but fades before he gains the altitude he needs.

The fourth updraft is a powerful one. Mermoz watches his altimeter climb and points his nose toward the pass. The current is strong and it lifts him safely into the pass. Ahead he can see a way open up through the mountains.

Suddenly he strikes a downdraft. Sharp fingers of rock reach up for him. Sheer cliffs speed past his cockpit as though he were in a glass elevator going down. The plane strikes something and rebounds into the air. Mermoz cuts the gas. The plane hits again and bounces down a rocky slope until it comes to rest on a tiny plateau.

Mermoz is uninjured. He glances into the back cockpit and sees that his mechanic, Collenot, is also unharmed. The two men climb out and are stunned by what they find. All around them is a jumbled disorder of cliffs, boulders, peaks, and canyons. The gently sloping plateau on which they have landed is the only flat surface as far as they can see. All is silent except for the sighing of the wind. Though it is midday, the temperature is 15 degrees below freezing and there are several inches of snow in spots.

Their first look at the plane is equally discouraging. The fuselage is smashed, the landing gear is broken, and the tail skid has been ripped off.

"Can we fix the plane, Collenot?" Mermoz asks.

"No, sir, I'm afraid not," the mechanic replies.

"Well, let's start walking!"

Stumbling and sliding in the rocks and snow, they head down a slope toward the west, figuring that their best chance of finding a settlement lies in the direction of Chile rather than Argentina. Overhead, three condors have arrived on the scene. The huge birds circle patiently, waiting for the mountains to deliver a meal to them.

After an hour of slipping and sliding, Mermoz and Collenot look back to see how far they have come from the plane. Less than half a mile! At this rate it is obvious that they will collapse from exhaustion in the high altitude or freeze to death before they can get very far.

"Collenot—we've got to repair the plane," says Mermoz.

"All right, sir, I'll try," says the mechanic.

They retrace their steps. Collenot studies the damage once again. "Maybe it will get us out of here," he says. "I'll get out my tool box."

With the three condors wheeling among the peaks to remind them of the price of failure, Mermoz and Collenot work through the afternoon and on into the night. There is a full moon, and in the clear air of the high altitude there is plenty of light. But the thinness of the air at this altitude exacts a toll—eventually Collenot's nose and ears begin to bleed. There is nothing to do but stop and try again in the morning. The men have no food or water and must eat snow to quench their thirst. Hungry and exhausted, they huddle together in the cabin of the plane to keep warm.

They work on the plane throughout the next day, but still it is not ready to fly. They spend another miserable night in the cabin, so weak now that they know they must get out soon or not at all.

At sunrise on the second morning, Collenot finishes bracing the fuselage and rebuilding the landing gear. "Now it's time to try the engine," he says. They start it up and it sounds good. But suddenly water streams from the radiator. The water has frozen during the two subfreezing nights, causing the radiator to burst. Mermoz shuts down the engine and Collenot quickly grabs whatever he can to plug the leaks—rags, pieces of wood, paper, even strips torn from his own pants and from Mermoz' leather flying jacket. Will it work? They dare not test the engine again. All they can do is pray that the plugs will hold long enough for one takeoff attempt.

While Collenot has been working on the plane, Mermoz has been intently studying the plateau and the surrounding peaks and canyons. The plateau lies at 13,000 feet. At this altitude, the engine will not develop enough power to make a normal takeoff. The plateau slopes downhill and this will help, but there are three sizable steps in the downhill slope, each of which could demolish the already shaky landing gear. Beyond the last step is a sheer drop-off to the canyon floor several thousand feet below. An audacious plan forms in Mermoz' mind.

The two men empty the plane of all its excess weight—spare gasoline, extra oil, tools, the seats in the passenger cabin. With their last ounce of energy they push the plane as far up the slope as they can.

They climb aboard. Mermoz starts the engine and gives it full throttle. Collenot shuts his eyes tight and says a prayer.

The plane gathers speed down the slope. It hits the first step. The landing gear holds. It is trying to fly now . . . the second step . . . landing gear still holding . . . the third step . . . the edge of the cliff is coming up . . . still not airborne . . .

As the plane rolls over the cliff, Mermoz points its nose down and it falls free. He holds it in a dive— down . . . down . . . down—until he gains flying speed. Slowly and carefully he pulls the nose up and starts a turn.

He has plenty of flying speed now and he gradually works his way out of the canyon. His desperate gamble has paid off. Luck is still with him. An updraft has him in its grip. He sails into the pass which had originally brought him into the heart of the Andes, and coasts down the green plains of Chile on the other side.

Mermoz arrived back at the field from which he had departed just as a search was being organized. He and Collenot had been lost in the Andes for more than two days, but they looked like they had been struggling against the mountains for weeks. Emaciated, frostbitten, and exhausted, they told their tale. The French pilots who knew Mermoz' skill and courage could believe it. But to most people, the idea of a pilot deliberately driving his plane over a cliff in order to take off was simply too fantastic. A short time after Mermoz' return, a Chilean expedition was sent to the spot where the plane had gone down. There, on the "plateau of the three condors," as Mermoz liked to call it, the expedition found the cabin seats and other items that had been jettisoned before Mermoz' dramatic takeoff. The incredible story had been confirmed.

Jean Mermoz (center) poses with the crew of another plane several years after his narrow scrape in the Andes.

The "Fastest Man's" Wildest Ride

The four-engined B-29 bomber spirals up toward 32,000 feet in wide, graceful circles. Strapped to its belly is a small, bullet-shaped rocket with short, stubby wings and a man inside. As the B-29 climbs with its strange payload, a countdown is going on between the B-29 crew, the ground tracking stations, two chase pilots flying F-86 jet fighters on either side of the B-29, and Major Charles E. "Chuck" Yeager, an Air Force test pilot, in the rocket.

"Approximately four minutes to drop."

"Roger, four minutes to drop," Yeager answers from the rocket.

"Liquid oxygen top-off procedure being terminated. Item three-seven-A."

A B-29 bomber with a strange passenger—Chuck Yeager's tiny X-1A rocket plane.

"A is complete and B is complete. Item three-eight."

"Three-eight complete. Can you disconnect the oxygen top-off, please?" the B-29 pilot calls to a crewman in the bomb bay.

"Right," the crewman answers. "The top-off fitting is disconnected and stowed," he reports a moment later.

"Okay, chase pilots." This is Yeager. "Liquid oxygen jettison valve is coming open."

"Good jettison," reports a chase pilot.

"Fifty—is five-zero complete, Charlie?"

"I will get it on the countdown," Yeager replies. "I am all clear to drop now."

"Okay. Building speed," says the B-29 pilot. "Thirty-two thousand feet now, two hundred and ten miles an hour. When I kick you out, you will probably be out about ten miles north of Victorville on a heading of two-eight-zero degrees. Building up speed now . . . got two-fifteen . . . got two-forty . . . now two-forty-five. Okay, Charlie. You give me the word for the countdown."

"Okay, Russ, start your countdown slowly."

"Roger, starting countdown, starting from five down to zero. Five. Four. Three. Two. One. Okay," he tells the copilot, "drop her, Danny."

The copilot pulls a lever and the rocket falls away from the B-29.

It is December 1953, and Chuck Yeager is going to try to fly faster than any man in history. In 1947

Yeager was the first pilot in the world to break the "sound barrier"—Mach 1. They called him "the fastest man alive" then. But in the six years since Yeager set his Mach 1 record, several pilots have pushed on beyond the sound barrier. Just three weeks before this attempt of Yeager's, a friendly rival, Scott Crossfield, reached a speed of Mach 2— twice the speed of sound—in a similar rocket plane. Yeager is determined to regain the title of "fastest man alive," but to do it he will have to fly faster than Mach 2 in his Bell X-1A experimental rocket plane.

There is nothing particularly special about Mach 2. It is simply a very high speed—about 1,650 miles per hour at 70,000 feet, the best operating altitude of the rocket plane. But there is one problem. Yeager's X-1A was not designed to fly faster than Mach 2. Since no one has ever flown at this speed, no one knows how Yeager's craft will react.

"Drop is okay," says Yeager. He flicks a row of switches one after the other to light off three of his four rocket engines. "Four and two are on . . . three coming on now."

The rocket drops below the bomber for a moment but its wings and airplane-like tail surfaces keep it flying straight and level. Then the rocket surges ahead. Yeager eases back on the control stick and points his nose toward the sky. At 45,000 feet he lights off rocket engine number one. With full power on, he arcs up to 70,000 feet and levels off.

"Got him in sight?" asks one of the chase plane pilots.

"No. He's going out of sight—too small," says the other chase pilot.

Yeager begins building up speed. The needle on the Mach meter moves steadily toward 2. The four rockets are screaming, but Yeager is flying much faster than the speed of sound and his cockpit is cool and quiet.

On the ground, Yeager's rival test pilot, Scott Crossfield, has joined the ground crew as they listen to the progress of the flight. The seconds tick by and the radio circuit is silent. "This is a good sign," Crossfield thinks. "It's just like Yeager to keep everybody on the hook."

Suddenly everyone seems to realize that too many seconds have ticked by without a transmission from Yeager.

"Chuck! Chuck! Yeager—where are you?" calls Jack Ridley, in one of the chase planes.

Yeager comes on the air, his voice weak and labored. "I'm . . . I'm down . . . I'm down to twenty-five thousand feet . . . over Tehachapi . . . don't know . . . whether I can . . . get back . . ."

"At twenty-five thousand feet, Chuck?" Ridley asks in amazement. Only seconds before Yeager had been at *70,000* feet.

"I'm . . . I'm . . . Christ!"

"What say, Chuck?" Ridley demands, hoping that his insistent voice in Yeager's earphones will

Yeager in flight in the X-1A.

help him hold on to his slender thread of consciousness.

"I say . . . don't know . . . if I tore . . . anything or not . . . but Christ!"

The worst thing that can happen to a test pilot has happened to Yeager. As he pushed the X-1A beyond Mach 2, it suddenly went wild. Its nose began oscillating left and right through an arc of 175 to 200 degrees per second. At the same time it rolled rapidly and tumbled end over end. The plane had gone beyond its limits and as the test pilots say, it "uncorked."

Yeager is rammed toward the ground. He falls about ten miles in 51 seconds. He is utterly helpless in a plane that is completely out of control. But on the fringes of consciousness his test pilot's mind keeps working. Thoughts race through his head: "There's nothing to hold to . . . the whole inner lining of the cockpit is shattered . . . the airplane rolls, yaws, and pitches . . . you don't know what hit you or where . . . it is like dying . . . there is nothing more you can do, no move you have strength enough to make . . . you've lost control, not just of your plane, but of your hands. You swear, you pray, and nobody hears a word, not even you . . . then slowly you come back to life . . ."

"Chuck, tell us where you are, if you can. Where are you, Chuck?"

"I think . . . I can get back to the base . . .

okay. Boy! I'm not going to do that any more!"

With those words everyone knows that Yeager is back in control again. The chase planes begin a frantic search to locate the rocket plane. Its engines are out of fuel now. It must be checked for damage and guided in for a dead-stick landing at Edwards Air Force Base.

Kit Murray in the second chase plane calls, "Chuck from Murray. If you can give me altitude and heading, I'll try to check from outside."

"I'm about . . . I'll be over the base at fifteen thousand feet in a minute."

"This is Murray, Chuck. I have you."

"Does everything look okay on the plane?"

"I am still catching up to you."

"Going to do a three-sixty-degree turn to left," says Yeager.

"I do not have you," says Murray. He had mistakenly homed in on another small jet in the area.

Now the old pro test pilot begins directing the show. "I am right over the end of a diagonal runway," says Yeager. "I am going to make a right-hand pattern. Gear coming down. Gear down and locked. Got me in sight yet, Kit?"

"Negative."

"Come down to twelve thousand feet on a right-hand downwind leg over the end of the east-west runway in the south end of the lake."

"All right," Murray reports. "I see him now."

Yeager squeezes into the X-1A. Lying on the ground is the plane's door—to be fastened in place when Yeager is in.

"Flaps coming down now," says Yeager as he completes his landing check list. "I am a little fogged up—not too bad."

"No! I don't have you Chuck!" Still another jet

has wandered into the landing pattern in the midst of the emergency, and Murray has mistaken it for the X-1A.

"I'm on the base leg. I'll be landing in a minute."

Kit Murray is still trying frantically to locate Yeager. Now the people on the ground can see Yeager heading toward the field. "Kit—swing to the right, sharp!" calls a pilot manning one of the radios on the ground. "Clear down on the edge of the lake!"

"Going to land a little long," Yeager reports. "I would appreciate it if you would get there and get . . . this thing off—this pressure suit. I'm hurting."

"Kit! He's right in front of you! Down below to the right!"

At last Murray lines up on the X-1A and talks Yeager down through the last few feet of the landing approach. "Coming off fifty . . . thirty . . . twenty . . . twenty . . . twenty . . . five . . . two . . . holding about two and a half . . . one . . . looks good, mighty fine."

The X-1A touches down and rolls to a safe stop, surrounded by an escort of fire trucks, an ambulance, and other emergency vehicles. In a few moments, Yeager is walking around the plane, bruised and shaken but feeling a lot better. He had flown Mach 2.5 and broken the record. He was still the "fastest man." But more important, he was still "the fastest man alive."

Harriet Quimby Flies the Channel

By 1911, just eight years after the Wright brothers' first flight, the new field of aviation was booming. Flying schools flourished in the United States, Britain, and continental Europe. The first air races were drawing enormous crowds and large numbers of pilots. New speed, altitude, and endurance records were being set almost every month as better and better flying machines appeared on the scene.

The first men who took to the air were thought of as death-defying, daredevil heroes. But a woman who wanted to fly was considered slightly disreputable. Women were expected to stay at home and "behave themselves." The strait-laced Wright brothers refused to enroll any women at all in their flying

32

school in Dayton. Claude Grahame-White, one of Britain's most famous fliers, declared: "I have taught many women to fly and I regret it. My experience has taught me that the air is no place for a woman. The truth is that women lack qualities which make for safety in aviation. They are temperamentally unfitted for the sport."

Even as Grahame-White was saying this, he was being proved wrong by a small but determined group of female pilots in France and the United States. Two Frenchwomen, Hélène Dutrieu and Marie Marvingt, were among the first pilots in Europe and had been setting records as early as 1909.

The American girls got a later start, but caught up fast. By the end of 1911, three American women —Harriet Quimby, Matilde Moisant, and Blanche Scott—had earned their licenses and were flying regularly in the United States. "Flying seems easier than voting," said Harriet Quimby, and in fact it was. The Constitutional amendment guaranteeing women the right to vote was not ratified until 1920.

Harriet Quimby was easily the most glamorous of the early women pilots. She was tall, green-eyed, and willowy. When she flew she dressed in a plum-colored satin flying suit with long fur gloves and high-topped leather boots. While still in her twenties she was drama critic and editor of the woman's page for *Leslie's Weekly*, a fashionable New York magazine. One evening, as she was working on an assignment for the magazine, she met some pilots who

were in town for a big air show. From then on she was determined to become a pilot, too.

In the summer of 1911 Harriet Quimby passed her tests and received the first official pilot's license issued to a woman in the United States. Hélène Dutrieu was the only other woman in the world who had an official license. Miss Quimby flew in the New York area for a while and made a barnstorming trip to Mexico with Matilde Moisant. But women aviators still weren't taken seriously—most newspaper write-ups devoted as much space to their flying suits as to their flying skill. So Harriet Quimby planned a flight that would earn the respect of other pilots and show the world what women fliers could really do. She decided to fly across the English Channel.

It's hard for us today to imagine that a flight across the English Channel could ever be considered a daring and impressive feat. The distance from Dover, on the English side, to the French port of Calais is only 22 miles. A modern jet takes less than five minutes to make the trip, and hundreds do so daily with less trouble than driving to the supermarket.

But it was a different story in Harriet Quimby's time. Those 22 watery miles looked like one great, wet graveyard to most early pilots. On a clear, calm day it might not be so bad. But the Channel is hardly ever clear enough of fog and mist to see from

Harriet Quimby in one of her controversial flying suits.

one coast to another. Calm days are likewise very few. The Channel's water is notoriously rough, choppy, and cold. To a generation of pilots who had learned from experience that their engines could easily quit every time they made a flight, the Channel was the last place they would choose for a forced landing.

The first flight across the Channel had been made in 1909 by Frenchman Louis Blériot, who said after landing that he didn't think he'd care to try it again. Two other French pilots set out to cross the Channel at the same time as Blériot. One was fished out of the water, uninjured but very agitated, shortly after he took off. The second decided his plane wasn't up to the trip and returned to Paris. By the time Harriet Quimby decided to try the flight, several men pilots had managed it successfully. But one very competent English aviator had disappeared without a trace on a Channel flight in 1910, and many more had simply decided there were better places to fly.

In early March 1912, Harriet Quimby went to Paris to arrange a plane for her flight. She picked out a new Blériot monoplane—the same type that Louis Blériot had used for his Channel flight. It was one of the finest aircraft of its day, but far from ideal for a flight out to sea. The cockpit was open and not even protected by a windshield. The engine had so little power that the plane couldn't take off if the wind was more than five miles per hour. In the air, the controls were so ineffective that it often took a pilot several tries before he could get a turn started.

The new plane was sent on to Hardelot, a little seaside resort on the French coast about 30 miles south of Calais. Since the Blériot was so tricky to fly, Harriet Quimby tried to get in some practice before setting out across the water. Each day she arose before dawn and went to the field where the plane was kept. But day after day high winds kept her from flying. So she shipped the plane to Dover, hoping that the weather would be better for practice on the other side of the Channel.

Sunday, April 14, was a perfect day for flying. The wind was calm, and from the airfield near Dover Castle, the young American could make out the hazy outline of the French coast in the distance. Her friends urged her to take off at once, but she made it a rule never to fly on Sunday. Bad weather set in again on Monday, but at 3:30 on Tuesday morning it seemed to the crewmen at the field that conditions were improving. They put in a call to Miss Quimby at her hotel. She quickly gulped a cup of hot tea and raced to the field. It was just getting light when the plane was rolled from its hangar and warmed up. The wind was calm and the sky was clear, although patches of fog still drifted in from the sea.

Experienced pilots advised that it would be cold crossing the Channel in the open cockpit of the Blériot, so the pilot dressed accordingly: two suits of

Miss Quimby climbs into a rickety Moisant monoplane.

long underwear under her satin flying suit, two over-
coats over the suit, and a wide sealskin stole over her
shoulders. At the last minute, someone handed her a
hot-water bottle, which she tied to her waist like an
enormous gurgling locket.

These were the *only* preparations she made for
flying the Channel. At 5:30 A.M. Harriet Quimby
took off for a coast she couldn't see through the fog
in a plane she had never had a chance to try out.
She had no maps, no instruments—except a com-
pass which she didn't know how to use—and no life
jacket or other survival equipment in case she came
down in the water.

She climbed to about 1,500 feet, then circled
back over Dover Castle so that a movie crew could
film her departure. The fog was thicker now; only
the top battlements of the old fortress loomed above
the swirling gray blanket. In an instant the Cliffs of
Dover were behind. The fog was thinner over the
water, and Miss Quimby spotted a tugboat that had
been sent out by a London newspaper to follow her
flight and help her if she was forced down. But up
ahead, the French coast was hidden by another wall
of fog that stretched as far as she could see in either
direction.

With no hesitation, she plowed right into it.
Moisture from the cloud bank drenched her plane
and dripped from every surface in the open cockpit.
Her goggles fogged up and she had to remove them.
The warmth of the hot-water bottle soon disap-

Aloft in the Blériot.

peared in the damp, penetrating cold. Unable to see anything, she flew on by instinct alone.

All great pilots seem to have a powerful inner feeling about flying. When the odds turn against them, their intuition takes over and they make the right moves without even thinking about them. So when the Channel fog closed around Harriet Quimby in her primitive monoplane, she simply flew on, guiding the plane as best she could until something told her she was near the coast of France.

Then she nosed over and began her landing descent. With the ground covered by fog and with no

altimeter aboard, she had no way of knowing how
close she was getting to the ground. Down, down she
went. Then suddenly the fog parted and she saw a
sandy beach below! She had arrived in France.

She flew back and forth for a while to find the
best place to land, then alighted on the beach. For a
few moments she was all alone. Then a crowd of ex-
cited fishermen rushed up. One of the fishermen's
wives miraculously produced a mug of hot tea and
some bread and cheese, and the men pushed the

French fishermen cheer Miss Quimby's arrival in France.

plane beyond the reach of the rising tide. In crossing the Channel in a flight that lasted a little over 30 minutes, Harriet Quimby had become the most famous woman pilot in the world. Someone in the crowd uncorked a bottle of champagne and raised a toast. As far as the French were concerned, that was all that was needed to make it official.

Oil Change Over the Tasman Sea

The year was 1935. High above the waters of the Tasman Sea, hundreds of miles from land, an old, ungainly-looking Fokker trimotored transport was flying east. Dawn was breaking and soon the sun would be rising. Inside the plane, its three crew members were hard at work. They had left Australia the previous evening and were heading toward New Zealand with the first official load of air mail ever to be flown over this 1,500-mile stretch of water. It was to be a historic flight.

Then trouble struck. Copilot P. G. Taylor was alone at the controls. Suddenly he noticed a small spot glowing white hot on the exhaust manifold of the center engine just ahead of the cockpit. He

The *Southern Cross*, Kingsford-Smith's Fokker trimotor.

quickly checked his engine instruments. Everything was normal.

Pilot Charles Kingsford-Smith was in the rear of the plane passing along some messages to the radio operator. When he returned to the front cockpit, Taylor pointed out the glowing spot with a nod of his head. The spot was bigger now. Suddenly there was a burst of flame, then a heart-stopping thud, and the plane began shaking as though an invisible giant were trying to tear it to pieces.

Kingsford-Smith's hand shot out to the engine controls and shut down the wildly vibrating right engine. When its propeller stopped turning, the plane stopped shaking. The two men looked out and saw what had happened. A piece of exhaust pipe from the center engine had broken off and flown back into the propeller of the right engine, snapping off one of its blades and throwing it severely out of balance. The plane immediately began losing altitude.

Exhaust flames still flared angrily from the broken manifold of the center engine. At this point, the plane was almost halfway across the Tasman Sea between Australia and New Zealand, one of the loneliest places in the South Pacific. Even today it's rare to spot a ship below when you make the 1,500-mile trip between the two "down under" countries by commercial airliner. But in 1935 there were no airliners on this run. With the right engine gone and the center engine acting up, the journey's end looked like it was going to be the open sea, with no help in sight.

It was a bitter moment for the two men. This was no ordinary flight—and these were not ordinary pilots. Taylor had been a combat pilot in World War I, then had returned to Australia to become one of the country's first airline pilots. He not only flew well, but was also a superb air navigator, perhaps the best in the world at that time. His specialty was pinpoint accuracy, using the sun and the stars for his fixes. His territory was the vast, trackless South Pacific, and he never missed when he had to find a tiny island on a long flight.

Kingsford-Smith was a national hero in Australia, an almost legendary pilot whose dazzling exploits included the first flight across the Pacific

Kingsford-Smith and co-pilot Taylor during a successful flight from Australia to the United States.

Ocean, the first nonstop flight across Australia, and
the first flight from Australia to New Zealand. He
had made all these flights in 1928 in a Fokker trimotor which he had christened the *Southern Cross* in
honor of the constellation that hangs in the sky over
the Southern Hemisphere.

The same plane was now faltering over the Tasman Sea. The *Southern Cross* should have been in a
museum. It was old, slow, and worn out. But Kingsford-Smith had a reason for using it on this flight.
One of the things he had hoped to prove on his earlier flights was that the airplane could help end Australia's long isolation from the rest of the world. But
in 1935 flying was still considered a dangerous sport
and the steamship was still Australia's main means
of contact with the outside world.

So Kingsford-Smith now turned to the public for
support. He announced that he would fly a special
air mail to New Zealand in the *Southern Cross*. The
response was enormous. Stamp collectors, school
children, and well-wishers of every kind sent letters
to be carried on the special flight—there were
29,000 letters in all. The *Southern Cross* was by no
means the best plane for the job—there were more
modern aircraft available—but it was a sentimental
favorite.

With one engine shut down, the old plane could
not stay in the air for long. Taylor made a quick cal-
culation of their position and reckoned they were
not quite halfway across the Tasman Sea. He scrib-

bled a new course to Kingsford-Smith, and reluc-
tantly the pilot turned west to try to get back to Australia. Taylor turned his attention next to the
problem: keeping the old plane in the air as long as
possible. "Have to dump some weight," Taylor
shouted above the racket of the straining engines.
"Should I go ahead?"

"Throw out everything but the mail," Kingsford-Smith shouted back.

With the aid of radio operator John Stannage,
Taylor heaved luggage, tools, and freight out the
cabin door. Still not enough! Next to go was excess
fuel. Taylor figured they were 600 miles from the
nearest land on the Australian coast. In its crippled .
condition, the plane was making only 60 miles per
hour; so Taylor saved enough gas for ten hours of
flying and dumped the rest. As the fuel streamed out
of the tanks, the *Southern Cross* stopped going down.
And none too soon—it was just 300 feet above the
waves.

Both pilots now settled down in the cockpit for
the long grind back to the Australian coast. They
were in radio contact with the airfield at Sydney
and they learned that rescue ships were steaming toward them from Sydney Harbor. But the ships were
many hours away. For five hours Kingsford-Smith
wrestled with the crippled plane. Then Taylor took
over the controls to give his pilot a break. The two
remaining engines still sounded healthy and Taylor
began to feel that the worst was over. He could even

throttle the two engines back slightly and relieve the strain on them without losing any more altitude.

Suddenly the needle flickered on the oil pressure gauge of the left engine. Taylor riveted his attention on the instrument. The needle fluttered again, then slowly began to fall below the normal reading of 63 pounds per square inch. It could mean only one thing—the left engine was running out of oil! When the oil was gone, the engine would stop.

Taylor attracted Kingsford-Smith's attention to the oil pressure gauge and the two veteran pilots looked at each other across the cockpit as if to say, "Well, it won't be long now." Taylor returned the controls to Kingsford-Smith and went back to the radio compartment to tell John Stannage of the latest trouble.

The radio operator immediately tapped out a final message: "Port motor only last quarter of an hour. Please stand by for exact position."

Taylor handed him the plane's estimated position, 34 degrees 8 minutes south latitude, 154 degrees 30 minutes east longitude, and Stannage sent it out.

When Taylor returned to the cockpit, the oil pressure in the left engine had dropped to 35 pounds per square inch. Kingsford-Smith was starting to take off his heavy flying boots so that he would be able to swim better.

What happened next was one of flying's greatest moments.

"Get the oil from the right engine. Go out and get it!" The thought flashed through Taylor's mind like a command. Seven or eight gallons of oil remained in the tank of the right engine after it was shut down. He had to get it and pour it into the left engine! It was their only chance.

Taylor belted his coat tightly and took off his shoes. "Going to have a stab at getting some oil!" he shouted. Kingsford-Smith tried to stop him, but Taylor already had one leg out of the window on the right side of the cockpit.

On the Fokker trimotor, the right and left engines were slung under the wings about five feet from the fuselage. The plane's nonretractable wheels were attached to long, spindly struts that stuck down from the engines. This arrangement was not strong enough to withstand a hard landing; so the landing gear was braced with a pair of tubes that ran from the wheels up to the bottom of the fuselage—and by an extra pair of struts that ran parallel to the wings between the fuselage and the engines.

With the 60-mile-an-hour slipstream tearing at him, Taylor groped for the parallel strut with his right leg and got his foot on it. He pulled himself out of the cockpit, got both feet on the strut, and braced his back against the front edge of the wing to keep from being blown away. He inched his way toward the dead engine, holding on to the cockpit with his left hand while he reached out with his right. Halfway out, and still too far to reach the engine, he had to let go with his left hand. With no handholds he was momentarily stranded. "I'm going in the sea anyway," he thought. "It's better to take a chance on reaching the engine." Resisting a desperate impulse to leap and grab anything he could, Taylor slowly sidestepped along the strut with his shoulders against the wing until he could reach the engine.

He looked back and saw Kingsford-Smith and Stannage gesturing to him to hurry. Taylor loosened the side cowling of the engine and it flew away in the airstream. Next he had to unscrew the drain plug in the oil tank. It was too tight. He tried to loosen it by hand, but it wouldn't turn. With a sinking feeling he realized that all the tools had been thrown out after the first engine had failed.

Again he looked back at the cockpit. Somehow, Stannage had found a spare wrench in the pilots' cockpit and was reaching it out into the slipstream. The combined reach of the two men's arms was enough so that Taylor didn't have to make the perilous return trip. He grabbed the wrench and loosened the drain plug until he could turn it with his fingers.

At this point Taylor had succeeded in the first half of his desperate mission. He had reached the oil tank on the dead engine and was ready to drain it. Now he had to figure out a way of getting the oil all the way over to the faltering engine on the left wing.

Stannage, the resourceful radio operator, was ready. Leaning out of the cockpit again, he held out an empty thermos flask which had contained coffee for the crew. Taylor grabbed it, loosened the drain plug, and let the oil run into the flask. The wind whipped at the oil as it drained out, splattering it against Taylor and depositing a slippery, treacherous film on the parallel strut he would have to use for his return trip.

The thermos flask was very small, holding only a few cups of oil. Once again, Stannage solved the problem. He emptied all the navigation charts out of a small leather suitcase, and each time Taylor passed him a flask of oil he emptied it into the suitcase. When it was full, he waved to Taylor to come in. Taylor inched his way back along the parallel strut, now slippery with oil, and made it back to the cockpit, where he collapsed on the floor.

This leather suitcase (fastened shut with a necktie) held the oil as it was transferred from one engine to another.

The oil pressure in the left engine was now down to 15 pounds per square inch. For a few minutes Taylor could hardly move, but the relentlessly dropping oil pressure meant only one thing: get oil to the left engine, fast! So Taylor started out the left cockpit window. He was immediately knocked back by the combined slipstream of the center and left engines, which were both running at full throttle. It took every ounce of strength Taylor had just to get his leg out the window, and then he could go no further.

The next move was Kingsford-Smith's, and it was a gamble that a lesser pilot would never have considered. He hauled back on the controls and took the staggering *Southern Cross* up to an altitude of 700 feet. Then he cut the left engine! The slipstream died away, and Taylor scrambled out onto the left strut. But with only the center engine running, the plane went down fast.

"Hold on," Kingsford-Smith shouted as Taylor reached the engine. Taylor wedged himself in among the struts, and the left engine came back to life with a roar. Taylor looked down and saw the crests of the waves just a few feet below.

Again, Kingsford-Smith hauled the plane back up a few hundred feet and throttled the engine back. Taylor tore off the oil cap. Stannage was ready with a full thermos of oil and reached it out to Taylor. With the wind whipping around him, Taylor could only get about half the oil from the thermos into the tank. But in a few seconds there were shouts and waves from the cockpit. The oil pressure was back up.

The plane was almost down in the sea again; so Kingsford-Smith signaled to Taylor to hang on and added power to the left engine. He climbed back up and throttled back once again so that Stannage could pass the remaining oil in the suitcase to Taylor. Again came a shout from Kingsford-Smith and the engine roared to life. The next time the engine shut down, Taylor scrambled back into the cockpit. The oil pressure gauge on the left engine was now steady at 63 pounds per square inch, and the exhausted, oil-drenched copilot sank down on the cockpit floor. Stannage radioed Sydney that the *Southern Cross* was still in the air.

Half an hour later, the oil pressure gauge on the left engine flickered again.

Wearily, Taylor once more inched his way out to the right engine, drained oil into the thermos, passed it back to Stannage, and then got it into the left engine while Kingsford-Smith climbed, cut the engine, and started it up again. This time they had to dump the mail in order to gain altitude—a bitter blow to the men who had hoped to win approval for a regular Australia–New Zealand air mail with this flight.

Taylor repeated this performance *five* times as the day wore on. Finally, about three o'clock in the afternoon, the pilots saw a low, purple streak on the horizon. Soon they could make out the low hills of the Blue Mountains along the Australian east coast. Taylor made his last oil transfer just 30 miles off the coast, and Kingsford-Smith brought the ailing *Southern Cross* in for a perfect landing at the Sydney airport before an enormous, wildly cheering crowd which had been following the suspense-filled flight through Stannage's radio reports.

When they landed, the center engine, which had given the first hint of trouble, was still running smoothly. It had not faltered once since its exhaust stack had disintegrated.

The Man Who Fell Up

Marine Lieutenant Colonel William Rankin locked his brakes and shoved his throttle forward. The afterburner of the F8U Crusader cut in with a clean, solid blast. "Feels good," thought Rankin. He released his brakes. The runway at the Naval Air station at South Weymouth, Massachusetts, began slipping past him faster and faster. Rankin felt his wheels leave the ground and pointed his nose toward the sky.

In seconds the powerful jet fighter was passing 10,000 feet, then 15,000 . . . 20,000 . . . 30,000 . . . 40,000.

"Tiger One, this is Tiger Two coming aboard your starboard side." Rankin looked over his shoul-

der and saw his wingman's Crusader sliding up in a
loose cruising formation.

"Roger Tiger Two. Full throttle. Boy, this is living!"

For the two Marine pilots, the flight was a wel-
come break from the intense training routine back
at their home base in Beaufort, South Carolina.
Rankin's wingman was a new pilot in the squadron.
They had flown into South Weymouth the day before as part of a final cross-country flight check for
the new man. Now they were heading home. It was
a gorgeous day in July 1959, and when they set out,
the sky stretched around them in a cloudless dome
that ranged in color from pastel blue near the horizon to the deep violet of near space above them as
they cruised at an altitude of 44,000 feet.

Their route was a straight line between the two
military airfields in Massachusetts and South Carolina. Traveling just under the speed of sound, they
estimated the trip would take them about 70 minutes. Shortly after takeoff they got a rare view of
New York on a clear day. Almost nine miles below
them, the sprawling metropolis looked neat and
well-organized. "It's geometry glorified," thought
Rankin as they sped by.

Now the New Jersey beaches unrolled beneath
them. As they passed Atlantic City the gemlike sky
became slightly shrouded with haze. They could see
patches of cloud stretching in increasingly dense
packs toward the south. At this time of year you

A Crusader jet similar to the one from which Lt. Col. Rankin ejected.

could almost bet on finding a monster thunderstorm at the mouth of Chesapeake Bay; in fact, the two pilots had been briefed to expect storms near Norfolk, Virginia. But the Crusader could easily outclimb even the mightiest summer storms, and all the weather forecast really promised for Rankin and his wingman was some spectacular cloud scenery as they flew over coastal Virginia and North Carolina.

Even so, Rankin felt he might have to push his jet a bit to get over one whopper that lay across their flight path.

"Tiger Two, this is Tiger One. Looks like Norfolk is catching hell. That's quite a storm down there."

"Sure is, Colonel," the wingman replied.

At 44,000 feet Rankin was beginning to encounter the wispy, ice-crystal tops of the storm. "Tiger Two, let's go into an easy climb to make sure we get over the tops," he said. He climbed up to 48,000 feet and leveled off in the clear once again.

Suddenly Rankin felt a thump and heard a rumbling sound toward the rear of his plane. He quickly scanned his instruments. All normal. Then came the thump and rumble again. A blaze of red light flashed on Rankin's instrument panel silhouetting four stark letters—FIRE!

Rankin throttled back. "Tiger Two, this is Tiger One. I'm having engine trouble. Stand by—I might have to eject."

"Roger Tiger One. If you have to go, let me know."

Rankin reduced his power and the fire warning light went out. But now he saw his r.p.m. indicator winding down rapidly from 90 percent power. Rankin was astonished to see it reach zero in five or six seconds. The whirling turbines of the jet engine had come to a complete—and sudden—stop.

"Engine seizure!" The thought raced through Rankin's mind. The crackling sounds in his earphones died out as the electrical generator stopped along with the engine. He tried his controls but

Lt. Col. Rankin demonstrates a model of his plane and his headgear after his adventure.

couldn't move them. The hydraulic system that supplied the power to move the control surfaces at near-sonic speeds also was driven by the engine, and when the engine stopped, the hydraulic system stopped, too. Rankin grabbed a handle that would activate emergency electrical and hydraulic power generators. He yanked and the handle fell loose in his hand!

There was nothing more he could do—and at any moment the plane might begin to tumble into a

screaming, spinning plunge from which there could
be no escape. He positioned himself securely in his
seat, reached up, and pulled two handles that
brought a canvas curtain down before his face.
There was a blast, then a tremendous kick, and in
an instant Rankin was catapulted from the warm,
pressurized comfort of his cockpit into the sudden-
death realm of the stratosphere.

The temperature in his cockpit had been 75 degrees; now it was 70 *below* zero in the thin upper air.
His body tumbled through the sky at several hundred miles per hour. His face and hands began to
sting and then froze and blessedly turned numb. He
spun and cartwheeled so violently that he could not
bring his hands close enough to his body to check his
parachute.

At the same time, Rankin was hit with the awful
agony of "explosive decompression." The difference
in air pressure between the cockpit he had just left
and the outside air at 50,000 feet was so great that
all the oxygen and other gases in his body expanded
suddenly, inflating him like a huge, misshapen bal-
loon. His abdomen swelled until he thought it would
burst. His ears ruptured, his eyes bulged from their
sockets, and his entire body was racked with intense
cramps. But in spite of everything, he was still conscious.

"Hang on," he thought. "Hang on—you might
make it yet. Just ride out this free fall and you've got
it made."

Rankin was plunging toward the earth at a speed of 10,000 feet per minute. If he could survive until he reached denser, warmer layers of air, his parachute would automatically open at 10,000 feet and get him to the ground safely. He entered the clouds at the top of the thunderstorm, still falling free.

In the moist, slightly warmer air in the clouds he began to feel better. How long had it been since he began his free fall? It seemed like an eternity, but his parachute still had not opened. Was something wrong with the chute? In the milky, darkening clouds he couldn't tell whether he was still thousands of feet above ground or only hundreds. He fought a terrible urge to pull the D-ring on his chute and open it manually. But his mind was still working well enough to know that if he opened his chute too soon he would freeze or die from lack of oxygen before he got down.

To Rankin's relief the parachute opened right on schedule at 10,000 feet. "Ten more minutes to go," Rankin figured, "and I'll be down." He slowly and painfully began to check his equipment. It was too dark in the clouds to see the parachute canopy overhead, but the two risers on either side of him were taut and steady. Now that he was at a lower altitude, the swelling and pain of explosive decompression subsided and his frozen extremities began to thaw. "I hope I won't land in a swamp," he thought.

But Rankin's ordeal was far from over. Suddenly

a shuddering blast of air jarred him from head to toe, then rocketed him upward again. Just as suddenly, a roaring downdraft rammed him into the raging heart of the monstrous thunderstorm that had towered beneath him when his engine failed. As helpless as a leaf in the screaming fury of the storm, he was slammed and beaten by the savage, tornado-like winds. At one point he found himself looking down into a long, black tunnel, a nightmarish corridor in space, it seemed to him. He shut his eyes.

The silken folds of Rankin's parachute whipped wildly as he was tossed up and down. At times he felt as though he were being thrown up and over the chute, loop-the-loop fashion, but somehow the lines remained untangled and his life-giving canopy did not collapse. All this time it was raining so hard that he could hardly breathe. Gusts of hailstones battered his flight helmet.

"The first clap of thunder came as a deafening explosion," he recalled later, "instantly followed by a blinding flash and a rolling, roaring sound that seemed to vibrate in my bones. I used to think of lightning as long, slender, jagged streaks of electricity—but no more. The real thing is different. I saw lightning around me in every shape imaginable. When very close, it appeared mainly as a huge bluish sheet several feet thick, sometimes stabbing close to me in pairs, like the blades of a scissors."

Minutes passed, then stretched to half an hour. "I'll never survive," Rankin thought. "What irony, to live through explosive decompression only to be battered to death by a thunderstorm!" But gradually the turbulence of the storm lessened and he could sense the clouds getting thinner. Finally he broke through the base of the storm in a heavy rain about 300 feet above a dense evergreen forest.

The parachute swept into the trees and Rankin came to rest against a tree trunk with a shuddering crash. For a few moments he lay there, stunned but still conscious. He moved a leg, then a hand, and cautiously sat up. His body ached and his face and hands were swollen and bleeding. But, miraculously, nothing seemed to be broken. He looked at his watch. It had taken him 40 minutes to make what normally would have been a 10-minute descent!

It was evening now, and raining slightly. Through the trees Rankin thought he could make out the lights of automobiles passing along a highway. He stumbled through the woods toward the lights and soon reached a road. He tried to flag down several cars but they wouldn't stop. He was a weird sight standing there waving wildly with his flight helmet, tattered flight suit, and battered face.

But one car slowed as it went by. In it were a mother and father and four boys. As they passed Rankin, one of the boys yelled to his father. "Dad! That's a jet pilot. He's in trouble. Stop! Help him!"

The car backed up. Rankin staggered to the window. "I'm a pilot," he gasped. "I've just ejected from an airplane. Take me to a hospital." The fam-

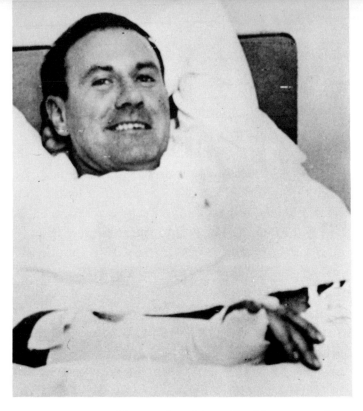

Miraculously saved from serious injury, Rankin recovers from frostbite and an injured hand in the hospital.

ily helped him into the front seat and headed for the nearest place to call an ambulance.

"Where am I?" Rankin asked.

"You're in Rich Square, North Carolina," the father replied.

In the wild 40 minutes that the storm had had him in its grip, it had carried Rankin 75 miles from the point where he had ejected. It was the most prolonged—and fantastic—parachute ride of all time. A few weeks later Colonel Rankin had recovered completely from his ordeal and was back in his squadron flying Crusader jets once again.

Across America, Crash by Crash

People were out on the streets of New York by the thousands. Down on the Battery, where Manhattan Island comes to a point, the crowds were so thick you could hardly find a place to stand. The same was true over in Brooklyn and along the boardwalk at Coney Island. It was a Sunday—September 17, 1911—but the streets swarmed with people because an airplane was about to fly over the city. Not only that—the pilot was going to fly all the way to California!

The plane appeared in midafternoon and the crowds went wild. As one reporter put it breathlessly, the flight was "the most daring and spectacular feat of aviation that this country or even the world has ever known!"

With its wings glinting gold in the slanting rays of the autumn sun, the plane dipped down over Coney Island, skimmed low over Brooklyn, and sailed in among the canyonlike streets of Manhattan. As it chugged uptown, the crowds in the streets could make out the words "Vin Fiz" painted in big letters on the undersides of the wings.

Finally the plane turned west over the Hudson River and gradually disappeared from view over New Jersey. For better or for worse, Cal Rodgers was on his way to "wash his wheels in the Pacific Ocean." In 1911 a pilot had to be crazy to attempt such a flight, and the people who watched Rodgers fly over knew it. But there was a powerful incentive for the flight. A prize of 50,000 dollars—a sizable fortune in those days—had been put up by the Hearst newspaper company for the first coast-to-coast flight in 30 days or less. And already Rodgers was behind. Six days earlier another pilot, Robert Fowler, had started working his way east from California, and four days before, an ex-jockey named Jimmy Ward had taken off from an island in New York Harbor and was now many miles on his way.

Rodgers's plane was a trim, custom-built Wright biplane, but it was never intended to make long flights. It had no cockpit, nor even a windshield. The pilot sat on what looked like a little stool up in front. The seat had no arm rests and no safety belt, and there was nothing to protect the pilot from the full force of the wind or rain or whatever else he ran

As Cal Rodgers takes off in his Wright biplane, spectators wave their hats in a good-luck salute.

into. In sporting circles, the odds were 50 to one that either the plane or the pilot—or both—would give up before the flight was finished.

Rodgers had an additional problem. He loved to smoke cigars and was never really happy in the air without a lighted stogie clenched between his teeth.

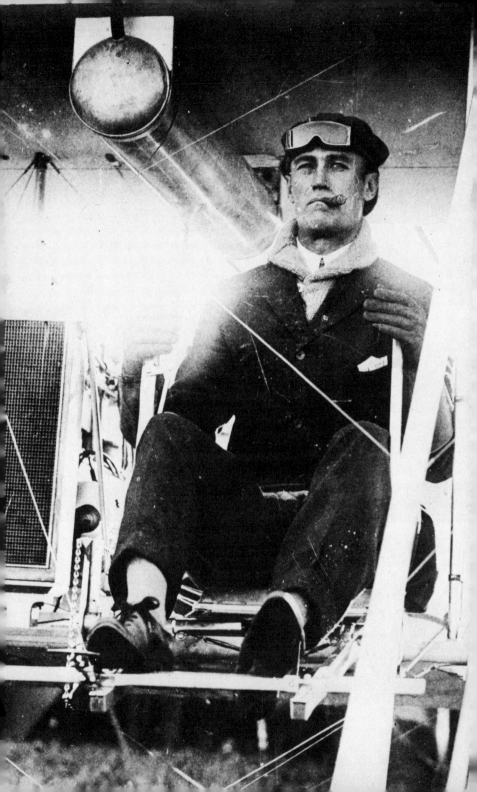

This made his flight very complicated. Somehow he had to manipulate the two control levers on either side of his seat, keep the engine running, hang on to his precarious perch, not get lost, and still keep his cigar lighted. Most of the time he managed pretty well, but occasionally, as we shall see, things got out of control.

After leaving New York, Rodgers followed railroad tracks in New Jersey until he spotted a special train that had been chartered to follow him all the way to California. The train was part of a deal Rodgers had worked out to pay expenses on the trip by advertising "Vin Fiz," a new grape soft drink. For every mile that he flew with "Vin Fiz" on his wings he received five dollars plus the use of the special train furnished by the soft drink company.

As evening approached Rodgers flew into Middletown, New York, to spend the night. It had been a most satisfying flight. "No man ever had a truer machine and a more perfect engine than I did today," said Rodgers. "I came down so easily it didn't knock the ashes off my cigar!"

But Cal's luck began to turn sour the very next morning. As he took off from Middletown he hit a tree and crashed into a chicken coop. Cal came to rest in a tangle of wire, wood, fabric, and chicken feathers, his head bleeding from a vicious clout on

Cigar clenched firmly between his teeth, Rodgers is at the controls.

the way down. Somehow he had managed to hang on to the cigar he had lit just before takeoff, but his plane was demolished.

The citizens of Middletown pitched in to help Rodgers rebuild the *Vin Fiz* flier. The Armory was thrown open for him, and the mangled aircraft and replacement parts from the special train were hauled there for reconstruction. Cal's mechanics worked around the clock and put the plane back together in 40 hours. Meanwhile, Cal's West Coast competitor, Bob Fowler, was getting set to cross the Sierra Nevada. Ex-jockey Jimmy Ward was having engine trouble in upstate New York, but was still far ahead in the race for the 50,000-dollar prize.

On his way again, Cal had some magnificent days of flying through New York. In setting down his thoughts for a New York newspaper, he was almost poetic about the thrill of flying in 1911: "I was above the air currents going faster than the wind and the engine went on singing a sweet song. I lit a fresh cigar and let her go.

"An airman cannot tell too much about the country he goes over. There are no signs up where he is and little towns come so fast that a new one seems to begin before an old one ends. All I could see was a ribbon of silver below me coiling around heavily wooded mountains. There was a glint now and then of the railroad tracks, but the river was my guide."

One day's flying, however, was cut short when a

spark plug fell out of his engine. Then there was the day he got lost. He landed in a farmer's field to find out where he was and a crowd materialized out of nowhere.

"They told me I was in Scranton, forty-five miles from where I ought to be," Cal said later. "The crowd went crazy and I had a hard time trying to save my machine.

"There wasn't a mark on my plane when I started in the morning, but in ten minutes, there wasn't an inch free from pencil marks. They didn't mind climbing up to get a good spot. They liked to sit in the seat, work the levers, and finger the engine. I nearly lost my temper when a man came up with a chisel to punch his initials on one of the struts!"

The crowd was basically friendly, though. They got him some gas and two men turned the props for him to start the engine so that he could continue on his way. On the same day, Jimmy Ward dropped out of the race. His engine was failing on every flight, and it wasn't difficult for his wife to convince him to drop out before he killed himself.

Rodgers's second major crash occurred at an Indian reservation near Salamanca, New York. He landed there one afternoon, and when he tried to resume his journey the next day he piled into a barbed wire fence on takeoff. He was uninjured, though, and got a good rest while the plane was rebuilt. Then he headed into Ohio.

In the meantime, Bob Fowler gave up his West-to-East attempt. He had tried three times to get his plane over the mountains, but couldn't get high enough. When Rodgers learned he was now the only prize contestant he drove himself hard across Ohio to make up for lost time. One morning the weather was bad, but Cal decided to take off anyway. Without meaning to, he suddenly became the first aviator in history to fly through a thunderstorm and live to tell about it.

One of Rodgers' crashes on his hazardous cross-country tour.

"I turned to the northwest," he wrote. "I noticed right ahead of me a full-grown rainstorm coming right at me. I saw the milky water falling and the clouds weaving. I turned and scooted to the east only to find another storm sweeping down on me. I had to turn and run away again, and this time I saw a third big cloud bearing down on me.

"There was a space between the two clouds and I made for it. It was clear enough, but I had forgotten the thunder and lightning. That was their little playground.

"The first thing I knew I was riding through an electric gridiron. I didn't know what lightning might do to an airplane, but I didn't like the idea so I swung around and streaked for the east again only to run bang up against a big rain cloud in active operation. I seemed to have run into a cloud convention.

"If you have been out in a hailstorm you know how that rain cut my face. I had taken off my goggles for fear that they might fog up and blind me, and I took off my gloves and covered the exposed parts of my ignition with them. It was a cold and painful situation.

"I looked for my engine to stop on me any minute and began searching for a place to alight. I couldn't find one because a big cloud had quietly rolled in under me and the earth had disappeared. It was lonesome. I might be a million miles up in space. I might be a hundred feet in the air. I breathed better when I sailed over the edge of the cloud and saw the misty land beneath me.

"I dropped down, landed all right, climbed under my machine to get out of the wet, and lighted a cigar."

When the rain cleared, Cal got back in the air and pushed on to Huntington, Indiana. The weather the next morning was still unsettled, clear but gusty. Rather than buck the gusts head on, Cal tried to take off downwind. Unable to gain altitude, he hopped and skipped across the field, then careened toward a group of spectators. Rather than plow into the crowd, he skidded his plane around, still desperately trying to become airborne. The *Vin Fiz* passed between two trees and under some telegraph wires. The left wing snagged on a small rise, the plane crumpled, and Cal was thrown completely clear of the wreckage. He was badly shaken but not seriously injured. His machine had to be rebuilt for a third time.

On Sunday, October 8, Cal finally flew into Chicago. He had been en route now for three weeks exactly and had covered only a little more than 1,000 miles. At this rate, it was impossible to reach California in time to win the 50,000-dollar prize. A Chicago reporter asked him if he was going to quit. "I am bound for Los Angeles and the Pacific Ocean," Cal said. "If canvas, steel, and wire together with a little brawn, tendon, and brain stick with me, I mean to get there. I'm going to do this whether I get

Legs dangling over the front of the wing, Rodgers passes a horse and buggy on the road below.

five thousand dollars or fifty cents or nothing. I am going to cross this continent simply to be the first to cross it in an airplane!" The odds were still against his making it alive, but Rodgers was determined to prove them wrong.

Cal's route now took him south through Springfield, Illinois; Kansas City, Missouri; Muskogee, Oklahoma, and on into Texas. He sped along as though he still had a chance for the prize, and all went well enough until the day he left Austin, Texas. Seventeen miles south of Austin his engine failed and he came down in a farmer's field. A piston had shattered and the entire engine had to be replaced with a spare carried aboard the special train. By now the strain of the journey was beginning to tell on Cal. He had lost 15 pounds since leaving New York and his leathery, windburned face looked "gaunt" according to a reporter who met him when he finally got to San Antonio on October 22.

On the day he left San Antonio Cal had another serious accident near Spofford, Texas. While he was trying to take off, his right propeller struck the ground. The plane swerved out of control and lurched to the left, splintering the propellers, demolishing the undercarriage, and crumpling the wings. Said Cal philosophically: "These wrecks are part of the game and are to be expected, but of course are unwelcome."

Cal averaged 142 miles a day across Texas when he wasn't grounded by bad weather. He still had plenty of troubles, but somehow the problems that caused such agonizing delays before Chicago could now be coped with more easily. On one takeoff, for example, he smashed his skids. But he repaired them in less than three hours and was still able to get in the best part of a day's flying. Another time his water pump began to leak and he smashed another skid during the emergency landing. Three hours later everything had been fixed and he was on his way again.

New Mexico was even better. It took Cal only one day to cover the 222 miles along his route through that state. He reached Phoenix, Arizona, on the morning of November 2, then literally flew on until his gas ran out. He landed at a small, one-man station on the Southern Pacific railroad, and when his special train caught up with him, it was too late to continue. So Cal and his party spent the night in the Arizona desert.

By now the end of Cal's odyssey was in sight. But the troubles that had plagued him across the continent so far suddenly seemed to intensify, as if in a last effort to prevent him from reaching his goal.

Cal crossed into California on November 3. As he flew over the Salton Sea his engine exploded, driving metal splinters into his right arm. Despite the pain, he made a perfect landing near Imperial Junction. It took a doctor two hours to remove all the fragments from Cal's arm.

The engine was hopelessly wrecked by the explosion, so Cal and his mechanics installed the old engine that had failed over Texas. On his first flight with the old engine Cal made only a few miles before he had to give up. His spark plugs came loose and the radiator sprung a leak. The mechanics got the engine running by the next day, but again Cal was forced down after only a few miles when a gasoline line broke.

Though Cal was determined to reach the Pacific Ocean, the "official" end of his journey was Pasadena, California. He finally reached Pasadena at 4:08 P.M. on the afternoon of Sunday, November 5. He had been en route 49 days since leaving New York and had covered 4,231 miles in 82 hours and four minutes of actual flying time, an average of 51.6 miles per hour.

Rodgers was mobbed by 10,000 wildly cheering people when he landed at a fair ground in Pasadena. He had to be escorted from the *Vin Fiz* by policemen who punched the crowd back with their nightsticks. Cal was wrapped in an American flag, driven around the field, then taken to a hotel, where he celebrated by drinking a glass of milk and eating some crackers. By this time there wasn't much romance left in flying as far as Cal was concerned. "I am glad this trip is over," he said. "Personally I prefer an automobile with a good driver to a biplane."

A week later Cal took off for Long Beach, California, on the last 30-mile leg of his journey to the Pacific. Halfway there, he crashed in a field while trying to make an emergency landing. Cal was hauled from the wreckage bruised and unconscious and was taken to a hospital.

The next day he revived, sat up in bed, smoked a cigar, and talked to his family and a few friends.

"I don't know what caused it," he said. "Something may have broken or I may have temporarily lost control. I can't say. Anyway I know I hit the ground a mighty hard whack. But it's all in the ball game. I am going to finish that flight and finish it with that same machine!"

Cal's ankle was broken in the crash and it was almost a month before he was able to fly again. Finally, on Sunday, December 10, he hobbled through an alfalfa field, climbed aboard the rebuilt *Vin Fiz*, tucked his crutches behind him, and took off for Long Beach. He landed on the sand and wet his wheels in the ocean as a gigantic crowd of 50,000 people cheered from the Long Beach boardwalk. It had taken him 84 days to reach his goal. "My record won't last long," he said. Then he made a radical prediction for that era: "With proper landing places along the route the trip can easily be made in thirty days or less."

Twelve weeks after taking off from New York, Rodgers finally wets his wheels in the Pacific Ocean.

Full Sail for Hawaii

The silence was heart-stopping. One moment the cabin of the big Navy seaplane was filled with the roar of two powerful engines. Then the roar was gone, leaving only the sound of the wind whistling through the struts and rigging wires of the biplane wings. As the pilot pushed the nose of the plane over, the whistling rose higher and higher in pitch in an eerie, discordant symphony.

A landing in the open sea was a serious matter, even for the sturdy PN-9, the Navy's finest flying boat in 1925. But the pilot, Commander John Rodgers (who had been aboard the special train when his cousin Cal had flown across the country in 1911), had been getting ready for it for some time. Since dawn he had known his fuel was too low to make it to his destination in Hawaii. As Commander Rodgers steadied the plane in its steep glide, he scanned the pattern of the waves and turned gently so that the plane would land parallel to the swell and not headlong into it. Back aft the radio operator tapped out one word three times: "Landing . . . landing . . . landing." Then he had to leave his set and brace himself for the touchdown impact.

Rodgers held the plane in its steep glide until the last possible moment. Then he leveled off. As his air-speed dropped, the hull of the plane skimmed the tops of the waves, then settled into the water with a spray of foam. The seaplane came to rest bobbing and rolling easily, a tiny speck against the vastness of the Pacific Ocean. It was a good landing. The four-man crew reported no damage or injury.

Though there were no ships in sight when he landed, Rodgers knew that several Navy vessels were not far away. He had been in radio contact with them before his fuel ran out. It would be just a matter of time before help arrived. Even so, the forced landing came as a great disappointment to Rodgers. Twenty-five hours earlier he had taken off from San Francisco Bay along with another sea-plane in an attempt to make the world's first flight to Hawaii. The other plane had been forced down with engine trouble just a few hours after passing the Golden Gate. It had to be towed back by a Navy ship which had seen it go down. Headwinds and

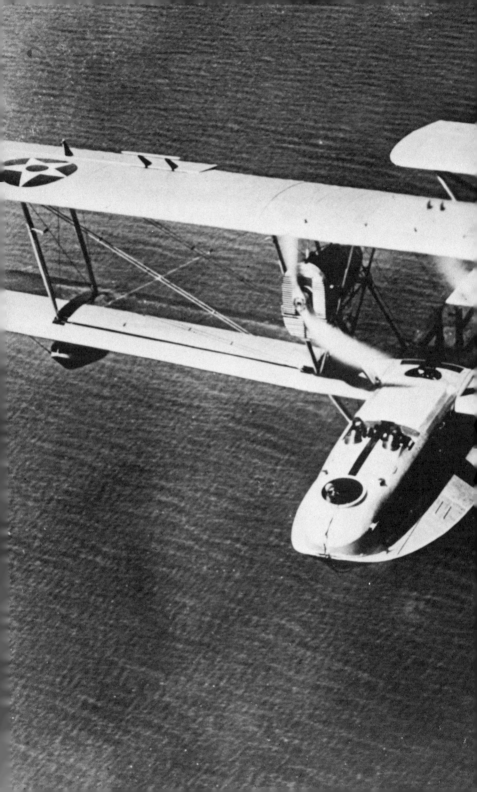

The Navy PN-9 seaplane flown
by Commander John Rodgers.

high fuel consumption had plagued Rodgers throughout his flight. Now that he, too, had been forced down, the honor of making the first flight to Hawaii would likely go to someone else.

Now there was nothing to do but call for help and wait until someone picked them up. Rodgers estimated that the nearest ship he had been in touch with, the Navy cruiser *Aroostook*, was only about three hours away. Rodgers' radioman unpacked a kite and sent it aloft with a radio antenna. But just as he started to tap out a message to the *Aroostook*, a gust of wind tore the kite loose from its line and the kite fell into the sea far from the plane. Now there was no way to tell anyone where they were.

They waited patiently throughout the afternoon and on into the evening, but nothing appeared on the vast horizon, which stretched all around them in a full circle. As night fell Rodgers turned on a light on the upper wing as a beacon and organized his crew into watches in case anyone should spot the feeble glow tossing in the immense Pacific blackness.

The horizon was still empty the next morning. The crew breakfasted on hardtack and cold canned beans. Again the radio operator tried to get out a message. This time he stretched a wire from one wingtip across the nose of the plane to the other wingtip. It worked fine as an antenna, but now the battery was too low to supply power to the radio transmitter and all he could do was receive messages. And all these messages did was make the crew feel worse.

For miles around them an intense search was going on. Rodgers' crew could hear the searching ships passing messages back and forth. Interspersed with these were calls to the PN-9:

"What is your position, PN-9?"

"Are you in distress?"

"If you copy our transmission, send us your position."

And over and over again, "PN-9, come in please."

The day wore on and still no ships appeared. At times the crew could tell from the strength of the radio transmissions that ships were incredibly close as they moved along search patterns designed to cover every square mile in the vicinity. But, incredibly, they kept missing the PN-9.

The radio traffic from the search continued on into the night. At one point, the *Aroostook* radioed:

"PN-9, PN-9, if you hear us, fire a star shell with your Very pistol."

Apparently the *Aroostook* had spotted something in the gloom. But it wasn't the PN-9. One of Rodgers' men fired a flare, and then a second, but still nothing happened.

On their third morning at sea, Rodgers decided he could wait for help no longer. Food and water supplies were running low and the longer the sea-

plane was in the water, the greater was the risk of its
going to pieces, especially if a storm or high sea
came up. Rodgers gathered his crew together and
told them:

"We're going to sail on into Hawaii!"

As a 1903 graduate of the Naval Academy,
Rodgers had trained on sailing ships as a midship-
man and had later gone to sea in just about everything the Navy had, from battleships to submarines,
before becoming a full-time Naval aviator. There
wasn't much about the sea he didn't know. Now,
under his direction, the seaplane was converted into
a sailboat. The crew stripped the canvas from the
lower wings and lashed it to the struts between the
wings. Slowly but steadily the PN-9 got underway
and began to pick up speed.

Rodgers and his navigator estimated their position to be about 350 miles east of the island of
Kauai, the westernmost major island in the Hawai-
ian chain. With the prevailing winds and currents
pushing them to the northwest, they figured they
had little chance of drifting into the other islands
that lay south of Kauai. And if they missed Kauai
there wasn't another island along their course for
thousands of miles. To make sure the wind did not
push them north of Kauai, Rodgers and his crew
tore loose the floor boards in the cabin of the plane
and lashed them to one side of the hull as a make-
shift keel. This arrangement decreased their side-

ways drift and enabled them to head about 15 degrees south of the course they had maintained without the keel.

By the sixth day, the emergency rations aboard the plane were almost gone. But even more ominous, the last of the water was gone from the canteens the crew carried. Mercifully, a rainstorm came up and, using a sail, the crew caught enough water to fill two canteens. Even better, they learned they had not

Unable to fly to Hawaii, the PN-9 sails in. The cloth on the near wing has been ripped off to be used as a sail.

been forgotten. From the *Aroostook* came this message:

"Cheer up, John! We'll get you yet. Use Very stars. Hammer hull so submarine will hear on oscillators. Use receiver as transmitter."

The radio operator tried once again to get a signal out. Two other crew members began beating on the hull with hammers. When darkness came, they shot off half a dozen Very flares. But still no help appeared. The next day passed uneventfully. That night, however, they saw searchlights on the southern horizon from an Army base on the island of Oahu. On the morning of the eighth day, Oahu itself was visible. The crew was elated, but Rodgers had to tell them the island was too far away to the south for them to reach.

The ninth day at sea was cloudy and misty at dawn, but by nine o'clock the weather had cleared and the crew could see the volcanic peaks of Kauai ahead about 40 miles away. After all this time Rodgers didn't dare hope to be picked up at the last minute. So he planned an approach to one of the two harbors on the rocky, volcanic island. Rather than risk a landing at night, Rodgers had his crew dismantle one of the plane's empty gasoline tanks and rig it as a sea anchor to slow the seaplane-sailboat down. While they were doing this, Rodgers built a fire in a bucket, using wing fabric as fuel, and sent up Indian-style smoke signals. The copilot tied another piece of wing fabric to the end of the pole and waved it from an upper wing.

Fifteen miles from Kauai on the afternoon of the ninth day, the American submarine R-4 finally spotted the PN-9 and came alongside. Fresh water and food were passed over to Rodgers' crew, and a towline was hooked up to the nose of the PN-9. As the seaplane was towed into harbor on Kauai, Rodgers and his men revived themselves aboard the sub with their first hot meal since leaving San Francisco. The PN-9 was safely anchored in the harbor by late afternoon. After a flight of 1,992 miles and a sea voyage of nine days, Rodgers had reached his destination in the same craft in which he started out.

After arriving safely, the crew waves to photographers in Hawaii. Commander Rodgers is at center.

The Race with Two Winners

On the Fourth of July, 1969, the big international airport at San Diego, California, was vibrating with excitement. Out on the field, 92 sleek light planes were warming up. Their wings sparkled with the high gloss of last minute polishing. Their finely tuned engines filled the air with an impatient buzz.

A few minutes after nine o'clock in the morning a single-engined Cessna with a big number 1 on its tail taxied up to a woman holding a flag at the end of the takeoff runway. The flag dropped and No. 1 zoomed down the runway and into the air.

The 23rd annual All-Women's Transcontinental Air Race—better known as the Powder Puff Derby —had just begun. From here on, it would be full throttle all the way across the continent to Washington, D.C.

A few planes back was Joan Steinberger of Goleta, California, in the TAR 10 position (Transcontinental Air Race starting position No. 10). The takeoff positions were determined by lot and Mrs. Steinberger was delighted to get off to an early start in her single-engined Piper Cherokee. Much farther back, Doris Bailey of Orange, California, was TAR 66 in a Cessna 172. Behind her, in the TAR 68 spot with a twin-engined Piper Comanche, was Mara Culp, also a Californian from Newport Beach. Of these three women, one would emerge as the surprise winner of the race and the other two would fail to finish because of a few minutes of high drama more than halfway across the country.

The first leg of the race stretched to the northeast toward Las Vegas, Nevada. The pilots scrambled for altitude as they left the green belt of coastal California behind them and headed for the bleak, barren mountains of the San Bernardino Range. Right at the beginning the fliers were faced with two of their most challenging problems—how to climb over the mountains without losing too much airspeed, and how to fly the most precise straight-line route to Las Vegas with very few prominent landmarks to guide them. Every second counted. The winner of the race would be the pilot who hit the highest average ground speed from coast to coast in relation to her type of plane; in past races, the difference between

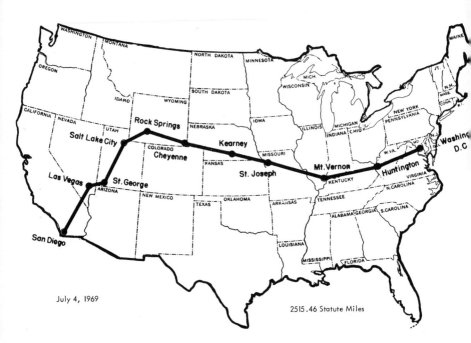

July 4, 1969

2515.46 Statute Miles

The route of the 1969 Powder Puff Derby.

first and second place was often a couple of minutes or less.

From Las Vegas the route of the race led through Utah to Salt Lake City, then arced eastward through the southern edge of Wyoming. It touched Colorado, crossed Nebraska, Missouri, and the southern tip of Illinois, then passed through Indiana, Kentucky, West Virginia, and Virginia to reach the destination, Washington, D.C.

The total distance was 2,515 miles, and despite its whimsical name, this Powder Puff Derby was no race for amateurs. Along the route the fliers would have to cope with every kind of terrain and every type of summer weather to be found in the United States. The rules didn't make it any easier—no instrument flying or night flying was permitted, the planes had to conform to rigorous safety rules, and their horsepower and equipment were limited in the interests of fair competition.

In addition, every woman in the race had to have at least a private pilot's license *plus* either an instrument rating or an instructor's rating. Though no American airline hired a woman pilot until 1972, there are hundreds of well-qualified women with thousands of hours of flying experience throughout the country. Many are flight instructors and many more routinely fly charter flights all over the United States. Joan Steinberger, for instance, specialized in flying emergency medical supplies to hospitals in California. Doris Bailey was a flight instructor, and Mara Culp was a charter pilot for a California aviation company. Some Powder Puff Derby racers even served as military ferry pilots.

As the fliers headed across the heartland of America, most of them decided to spend a night at St. Joseph, Missouri, one of the Derby's officially designated stopover points. Joan Steinberger was one of these. On the morning of Monday, July 7, she got out to the airport early and prepared her Cherokee for a full day at top speed. But when she checked the weather, she wondered if she would get in a full day's flying after all. Already thunderstorms were reported building up throughout a wide area on either side of the route to the next checkpoint at Mt. Vernon, Illinois.

"I might as well push on through and see how far I can get," she thought to herself as she filed her flight plan.

The pilots leaving St. Joseph that morning began to encounter the first thunderstorms after they crossed the Mississippi River in the neighborhood of St. Louis. At first the storms were scattered and all that was needed to avoid them was a slight detour now and then. But they looked ominous to Mrs. Steinberger as she neared the field at Mt. Vernon. The sky around Mt. Vernon was dark, almost black near the ground, and the dense clouds at the edge of the storm had a solid, rolling look that Mrs. Steinberger knew meant high winds and severe turbulence far beyond the strength of her little plane.

As Joan Steinberger approached the field from the northwest, she called the Mt. Vernon tower. The news was bad.

"TAR ten, this is Mt. Vernon tower. The field is below minimums. Visibility one and one-half miles in heavy rain. Hold south of the field and await further instructions."

A minimum of three miles visibility and a cloud ceiling of at least 1,000 feet is required by law before a plane can land at any airport unless it uses an instrument approach. Since instrument flying was forbidden by the rules of the Powder Puff Derby, Mrs. Steinberger had no choice but to remain clear of the field until visibility improved enough to land.

At the field itself, air traffic controller Charles Thomas was having a difficult day. His "tower" was a pickup truck with radio equipment in the back. The Mt. Vernon airport was a small one and had no conventional tower facilities; so Thomas had been sent over from a large airport at nearby Evansville, Indiana, with temporary equipment to help the pilots on their way. As he stood by the truck, the wind-whipped rain lashed at him and the lightning crackled in his headset. But that wasn't the worst thing. Thomas was impressed by the skill and competitive spirit of the women who had already passed through Mt. Vernon and he knew that every minute he made the new arrivals wait would reduce their chances of winning. There was nothing he could do, though. As long as the heavy rain continued to reduce the visibility, no plane could legally land.

Joan Steinberger followed the tower's instructions and turned south. Soon she passed over a prominent dual highway which gave her a good landmark to circle while she waited.

Mrs. Steinberger wasn't the only one in the air around Mt. Vernon, however. As she circled south of the field, she heard one of her competitors call in.

"Mt. Vernon tower, this is TAR sixty-six. Can you give me a radio bearing to the field?"

"That was odd," Mrs. Steinberger thought. "She must be having some kind of trouble if she needs directions to the field."

"TAR six-six this is Mt. Vernon tower. Unable to give you a bearing. We don't have the right equipment."

"Mt. Vernon tower, this is TAR sixty-six. Can you give me a steer? Over."

The tower repeated its message, but back again came the same request from TAR 66 for directions to the field. For some reason, TAR 66 was unable to hear anything the tower was saying. "This could be serious," Mrs. Steinberger thought as she listened in on the radio transmissions. She scanned the dark, storm-whipped clouds that boiled around the Mt. Vernon airport, but there was no sign of the other plane.

The storm and the terrain below had sprung a trap on Doris Bailey in TAR 66. Normally the course between St. Joseph, Missouri, and Mt. Vernon would have been a straight line. But Mrs. Bailey had discovered severe storms lying directly across the straight-line course. She had turned aside to try to get around the fast-moving storms, but they had closed in behind her, and she was forced to wander farther and farther from her course to remain clear of the clouds.

As Mrs. Bailey dodged the clouds, she searched the ground for landmarks with which she could fix her position on her map and work her way back to the airport. But in southern Illinois and nearby Indiana, everything on the ground looks very much the same, even on a clear day. This is beautiful, flat farm country and for miles in any direction, a person in an airplane can see few things that stand out as landmarks. Nearly all the country roads run in straight lines from north to south and east to west, the towns are all about the same size and shape, and the little winding rivers all look alike. With the sky darkened by the storm, it was all but impossible to pick out points on the land below and identify them on a map.

With each passing minute, the needle of Mrs. Bailey's gas gauge moved slowly but relentlessly toward the "empty" mark. Airport or no airport, she would soon be down. Again she called for help.

This time Mrs. Steinberger answered. "TAR sixty-six, this is TAR ten. Can you read me?"

"Roger, TAR ten."

"The tower can hear you but they can't give you a steer. No equipment. Try to tell me where you are and I'll relay the message for you."

"I'm in the clear above a highway and a railroad. I can see a tower of some sort."

Mrs. Steinberger repeated the message to the traffic controller at Mt. Vernon. On the ground Charles Thomas mentally reviewed the surrounding countryside which he had flown over many times, but he couldn't quite visualize the landmarks Mrs. Bailey had described.

"Tell her to keep circling and call in anything else she sees," Thomas radioed to Mrs. Steinberger.

A few minutes later Mrs. Bailey described a river

Joan Steinberger and her Piper Cherokee.

and mentioned that she saw smoke from some sort of factory or power plant. When this was relayed to Thomas he could picture the scene.

"Tell her she's over the Wabash River now,"

Thomas called to Mrs. Steinberger. "She can probably contact Evansville tower." Thomas read off the
Evansville radio frequency to Mrs. Steinberger and
she relayed the information to Mrs. Bailey. Mrs.
Steinberger tuned in Evansville herself and stood by
to see if she could be of further assistance, even

though every extra minute in the air would reduce her chances of winning the race. After a while she heard TAR 66 make radio contact with the tower there and receive landing instructions. When Mrs. Steinberger was sure Mrs. Bailey was safely on the ground, she threaded her way through the thunderstorms back to Mt. Vernon, found the field was clear, and landed.

The incident took only 20 minutes and Mrs. Steinberger, Mrs. Bailey, and Charles Thomas made it sound almost routine. But routine it definitely was not. Mrs. Bailey's plane ran out of gas as she touched down at Evansville. And by spending so much time in the air to help a competitor, Mrs. Steinberger had sacrificed all chances of winning.

When the race was over and all the times computed, Mara Culp, TAR 68, was announced the winner. She made the 2,515-mile trip in 11 hours and 57 minutes—an average of 210 miles per hour. It was the very first Powder Puff race for Mrs. Culp, and a great personal triumph for her. A native of Soviet-controlled Latvia, she had come to the United States, learned to fly, and married her flight instructor. Now she had won the toughest and most professional women's air event in the world.

Joan Steinberger and Doris Bailey could not finish the race because continuing bad weather prevented them from completing it by the official deadline. But in the hearts of pilots everywhere, men and women alike, the flier who gave up the race to help a comrade in distress was a winner, too. As President Richard M. Nixon wrote to Mrs. Steinberger in a personal letter: "Nothing represents more clearly the purpose of this kind of contest than the outstanding sportsmanship you displayed when you went to the aid of another. Congratulations!"

The winner of the Derby, Mara Culp (center), and the mother-daughter team that finished second, Carol Simons (left) and Virginia Wegener.

Left Behind in the Arctic

The runway was a groove in the ice with walls of
snow heaped up on either side. As the small, single-
engined Lockheed *Vega* gathered speed, it careened
from side to side, missing the snow banks by inches.
It lurched into the air, dropped back on its skis momentarily, then bounded clear of the ice. In the navigator's compartment, expedition leader George Hubert Wilkins wrote a note and passed it forward to
the pilot: "Wonderful takeoff. How's everything?"

"Everything great!" pilot Carl Ben Eielson
shouted back through a speaking tube which was the
only way the two-man crew could talk and be heard
above the roar of the engine.

In a few minutes they were above the Arctic

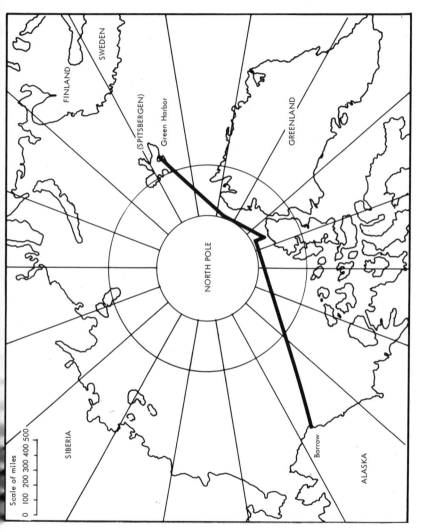

The Wilkins-Eielson route from Barrow, Alaska, to Spitsbergen.

Ocean heading toward the North Pole. If all went
well, their flight would take them from Point Barrow
on the north coast of Alaska to Spitsbergen, a large,
blizzard-whipped Norwegian island outpost 2,200
miles away on the other side of the world. But both
men were experienced Arctic fliers, and they knew it
was foolish to expect everything to go according to
plan. In fact, at the time of this flight in 1929, simply
getting off the ice at Point Barrow without crashing
was cause for celebration.

As the land dropped farther behind them, Wilkins and Eielson looked out on parts of the Earth
that no one had ever seen before. Other expeditions
had reached the North Pole by dog sled over the ice,
and Admiral Richard E. Byrd had flown over the
Pole three years earlier. But vast stretches were still
unexplored and many questions remained unan-
swered. Was there any land at all near the Pole? Or
was the Arctic all a frozen ocean, as most scientists
and explorers believed? Was it an impossible waste-
land of ice throughout or were there smooth places
where a plane could land in an emergency?

No one had ever risked such a long flight over
the Arctic. But this crew was well prepared to make
the attempt. George Hubert Wilkins was one of the
most renowned polar explorers of his time. He had
become impatient with footslogging along behind
dog teams during several long overland expeditions
from 1914 through 1922. So he had taught himself

aerial navigation and had learned to fly, although he was not a licensed pilot.

To actually handle the plane on the trip, Wilkins had selected the best pilot in Alaska, Carl Ben Eielson, a strapping American of Viking descent who had learned to fly in the Army. Together the two experienced Arctic hands had crammed every inch of available space in the six-place Lockheed Vega with extra gas and oil tanks plus enough survival equipment to enable them to walk to safety if they were forced down. The cabin of the plane was so crowded, in fact, that Eielson, alone in the front cockpit, could not see Wilkins at his navigator's table in the main cabin. They could only communicate by using the speaking tube and by passing notes back and forth around a large gas tank that blocked the passageway.

To survey the greatest extent of unexplored territory, Wilkins had plotted a route that skirted the North Pole, then curved toward the northern tip of Greenland where he hoped to sight land and fix a position with bearings. Wilkins estimated that it would take roughly 20 hours to fly from Point Barrow to Spitsbergen—and it was these long hours, rather than the great distance, that presented the greatest danger. In minutes a clear day in the Arctic can be blotted out in a howling blizzard. A favorable tailwind can switch without warning to a disastrous headwind, and every Arctic pilot flies with the uncomfortable knowledge that the weather may completely close down the place where he wants to land by the time he gets there. The longer the flight, the more likely the weather is to go bad, and on a flight of 20 hours, bad weather is almost guaranteed somewhere along the route.

The pale April sun hung low on the horizon as Wilkins and Eielson worked their way north. Ahead of them, hour after hour, the sky remained a clear, steely blue. As far as the eye could see, the Arctic ice pack was a chaotic landscape of heaped and broken ridges, evidence of the tremendous pressures that build up when ice floes are jammed together by high winds and churning ocean currents. There was no safe place for an emergency landing among these jagged blocks. And no evidence of land, either.

The first signs of bad weather appeared in the eleventh hour of their flight. Wilkins noticed a darkening in the sky behind them, then an odd grayness, scarcely visible at first, up ahead. Apparently a storm system had moved in quickly behind them and another was forming ahead of them in the vicinity of Greenland. Soon they reached the fringes of the Greenland storm. They began climbing as the clouds rolled in below, completely obscuring the surface.

Sighting land along the Greenland coast was critical for their navigation. The Arctic plays some strange tricks with navigation equipment. Magnetic compasses can point south to indicate north. Celes-

Wilkins and Eielson take off from Alaska.

tial navigation fixes with a sextant can be wrong by
as much as 100 miles when the sun is low on the horizon. Drift meters can make no estimate of wind direction and speed when the ground is blanketed
with clouds. Wilkins was a good navigator, but he
knew that any one of these variables could make
them miss Spitsbergen completely unless he was able
to pinpoint their position at Greenland before pro-
ceeding on the last long leg of the journey.

Eielson had to weave more and more between
towering banks of clouds in order to stay in the
clear. Suddenly, above the roar of the engine, there

was a shout from the front cockpit. Wilkins looked out and saw mountain peaks jutting up through the clouds. For a few minutes, the clouds parted below them and they could see enough of the coast to fix their position. When Wilkins had made his calculations, Eielson corrected the plane's course, steering it directly toward Spitsbergen. Their exploratory work was over—the rest of the flight would be over a well-charted region of the ocean. Now all they had to do was find a safe place to land.

Wilkins poured himself some coffee from a thermos and ate some dry biscuit while he considered what to do next. The wind was strong, and from the west the temperature had dropped to 40 degrees below zero outside the plane. The men could see storms over Greenland and a darkening sky in the direction of Spitsbergen. These signs led Wilkins to one conclusion: they would find heavy clouds over Spitsbergen and perhaps a violent storm.

He wrote Eielson a note: "We are above storm now. Down there we can land and wait until it's over. Can we get off again? If we go on we will meet a storm over Spitsbergen and perhaps never find the land. Do you wish to land now?"

"I'm willing to go on and chance it," Eielson replied.

For two hours they flew on in the clear. Clouds billowed below them, and a wall of towering cumulus clouds ahead of them reached higher than the plane could fly. Still, Eielson was able to thread his way between the cloud banks and maintain his course. The air was turbulent, and the little plane, with most of its gas gone, tossed and bucked violently in the increasingly strong winds.

But Wilkins' navigation had been perfect and Eielson's piloting superb. In the twentieth hour of their flight, two jagged peaks appeared below them in a break in the clouds—Spitsbergen! Eielson nosed the plane over and guided it around the mountain tops until he was able to slip under the clouds along the coastline. A dark and gloomy scene greeted them. The sun was obscured by the thick layer of clouds. A furious wind whipped the sea into angry crests and filled the air with salt spray. Ashore, blowing snow snaked along the ground in long, sinuous wisps that piled up in high drifts whenever they hit an obstruction.

They turned inland. A smooth patch of snow-covered land flashed by them, but Eielson missed it. Wilkins guided him back to it again. Again Eielson flew past the smooth area, but this time he saw it and circled. He leveled his wings and began to descend into the swirling snow, unable to see anything as he got close to the ground. He lowered the plane gently until the skis kissed the ground. The wind was blowing so hard that the plane traveled only 30 feet after touchdown.

Wilkins hurried out to cover the engine and drain the oil before it froze. Eielson joined him and they stamped snow around the skis so that it would freeze and prevent the plane from turning over in the high wind. The two men then climbed back into the cockpit, shared the last remaining hot coffee, and settled down to await the end of the storm. The plane rocked and trembled in the gusts and soon Wilkins and Eielson fell asleep. They had reached their destination, but their journey wasn't over yet.

Several hours later the storm ended and the two men awoke to find the sun shining. Their first problem was to determine exactly where they were. With the emergency equipment they had aboard the plane, they could either restart the engine and fly out if they had enough gas to reach the nearest settlement, or they could walk out, fishing through the ice and shooting game for food. But where was the nearest settlement?

Wilkins and Eielson strapped on skis and trekked over to a small rise. Wilkins scanned the horizon through his binoculars and searched the mountains and valleys to the east. Far in the distance he thought he saw the houses of a village. But the image danced and wavered and Wilkins knew he had been deceived by a mirage. He tried to fix his position with a sextant observation of the sun, but with no luck as the wind sprang up again, and the two men had to hurry back to the plane before they lost sight of it in the blowing snow.

Only careful preparation and warm clothing allowed Eielson (left) and Wilkins to survive their ordeal.

They had landed on a Monday, and it was not until the following Friday that the weather cleared enough for them to think seriously of trying to reach civilization again. The plane's cabin was cozy enough, there was plenty of food, and their sleeping bags and fur-lined flying clothes kept them warm enough. While they waited, they measured the fuel remaining and found they had 20 gallons left, enough to take them anywhere they wanted on Spitsbergen. So they decided to fly out when the weather broke. All day Friday they packed snow down in front of the plane for a takeoff runway. At three o'clock on Saturday morning, in the wan light of a cold sun low on the horizon, they cut the ice away from the plane's skis, lit a special stove under the engine to warm it up, and began heating engine oil over their cooking stove in the cockpit.

When all was ready, Wilkins swung the propeller. The engine roared to life without a miss and he climbed back in the plane. Eielson gave the engine full throttle—and nothing happened! Light as it was with so much of its fuel gone, the plane still remained stuck to the ice.

Wilkins got out and pushed the tail to get the plane moving. It leaped ahead as Eielson gave it full throttle. Wilkins grabbed for the cabin door but missed and fell in the snow. The plane bounced along the ice, gathered speed, and took off, leaving Wilkins behind.

Because of the way the pilot's and the navigator's cockpits were arranged, Eielson didn't realize he had taken off without Wilkins. The gas tank between the two compartments made it impossible for Eielson to see what was going on behind him unless he unstrapped himself and got out of his seat. So he flew on, unaware of what happened.

He was never able to say what made him put the plane into a turn. But for some reason he banked around as he was gaining altitude. He spotted Wilkins waving to him. Eielson came back and landed.

The plane still had to be pushed in order to get off. This time Wilkins unpacked a rope ladder from the emergency equipment, thinking that if he could get the plane moving and get a foothold in the rope ladder, he could climb in the cabin door as the plane left the ground. Eielson revved up the motor, and Wilkins gave another push and grabbed the rope ladder. It whipped back and forth as the plane gathered speed. Wilkins' hands were now too numb to hold on, so he grabbed the rope with his teeth. Just as the plane was about to leave the ground he realized he could never reach the cockpit this way; so he let go. He hit the tail of the plane, then dropped into a soft snow bank.

Once again, Eielson circled back and landed. Wilkins was stunned by this fall, but not injured. They had to make it this time. Fuel was running low. It would have meant certain death to leave one man behind on the ice even if he was left with all the emergency equipment aboard. If the two of them stayed, they would have to abandon the plane and strike out over land, hoping to find some settlement.

For the third attempt, Wilkins picked out a pole from a nearby tangle of driftwood. He thought he could brace himself in the cockpit door and push with the pole just enough to get the plane moving. To help get a better start the two men raised the plane's tail into flying position and rested it on a block of ice. Wilkins settled in the cabin door with the pole in his hands and Eielson gave the engine full throttle. For a full minute nothing happened. Then the plane broke free and began its takeoff run. Wilkins pulled himself all the way aboard and tumbled to the floor of the cockpit, completely exhausted.

Just as Wilkins recovered to the point where he could begin to think again about their position, Eielson called out, "What's that over in the bay to the left?" Wilkins looked out and saw two tall radio towers and a group of houses. "Go over and land where you think best," he told Eielson. They crossed five miles of open water, swung around a mountain top, eased down to a landing on smooth ice at the foot of the radio masts, and found they had arrived at Spitsbergen's largest settlement.

Their incredible journey was finally over.

The little Lockheed Vega, its engine covered to protect it from the cold, is examined by residents of Spitsbergen after its safe arrival.

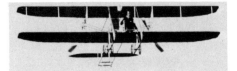

The Plane that Couldn't Land

The night of February 21, 1961, had been a busy one in the radar room of Washington Approach Control. A blanket of fog and low clouds hung over most of the Atlantic coast, and all traffic coming into the Washington area for landing was on instruments. By ten o'clock, though, the moving dots of light on the radarscopes were growing fewer as the evening rush hour slacked off at Washington National Airport, the capital's busy main terminal. The traffic controllers who hunched over the radarscopes in the darkened room could relax a bit.

In addition to the airline traffic coming into National Airport, Washington Approach Control also handled incoming flights to several military fields.

118

One of them was Anacostia Naval Air Station, just across the Potomac River from National Airport. It was a quiet night at Anacostia. The status boards at Approach Control listed only one flight inbound to the Navy base. It checked in on schedule over the Washington radio range station.

"Washington Approach Control, this is Navy four-oh-three-seven-eight. Washington range station on final for Anacostia."

"Roger, Navy four-oh-three-seven-eight," replied the controller. "You are cleared to land at Anacostia. Ceiling reported five hundred feet, visibility one and one-half miles. Wind calm."

The controller glanced at the information he had on Navy 40378. It was a twin-engined Convair transport plane almost identical to the type used by many airlines. The controller noted with interest that there was a high-ranking government official aboard and he wondered who it was.

The blip of light that represented Navy 40378 moved steadily on into Anacostia on the controller's radarscope. But when the blip reached the spot that marked the field, it kept right on going. Navy 40378 had not landed.

The controller beckoned to his watch supervisor. It was a bit unusual for a plane not to land at the end of an instrument approach, but not necessarily a cause for alarm.

"Navy four-oh-three-seven-eight, we have observed your missed approach," said the controller.

"Turn right to heading one-eight-zero degrees for radar vectors back to approach course for Anacostia."

There was no answer from Navy 40378. The controller and his supervisor watched the radarscope intently to see what would happen next. The plane did not turn. They called again, but the moving dot of light continued on straight ahead. Clearly, something had gone wrong.

Meanwhile, up in the cockpit of Navy 40378, three men were battling in utter blackness to keep the plane in the air. Just before reaching Anacostia, a one-in-a-million equipment failure had knocked out all electrical power. All the radios had gone silent and all the lights had flickered and died in the cockpit. Even more critical was the loss of all primary navigation equipment and all radios. Without these instruments, pilot Harry E. Patterson could not tell where he was and there was no way for him to let down to a safe landing through the fog. Without radios he could not tell air traffic controllers on the ground what had happened, he could not receive emergency instructions, and he could not find out how to avoid any other planes that might be groping through the fog along the high-density approach corridors to Washington. Navy 40378 was truly a derelict in the sky, and a menace to every other plane flying that night.

There was intense activity in the cockpit, but no panic. Failures like this were never supposed to hap-

A twin-engined Convair transport similar to Navy 40378.

pen. Nevertheless, the crew of Navy 40378 knew exactly what to do. Copilot Martin Denton flipped a switch to turn on a small emergency generator that operated off one engine independently of the main electrical system. That restored two vital instruments on the copilot's side—the gyro horizon and an electrically-powered turn-and-bank indicator.

But Patterson still couldn't see the instruments. He struggled to hold the plane level, but his sense of balance betrayed him in the darkness.

"You're dropping off!" the flight engineer yelled above the roar of the engines. The flight engineer fumbled in the darkness and came up with two flashlights. With his left hand he focused a beam on Patterson's instrument panel; the light in his right hand stabbed out toward the copilot's panel.

Patterson righted the plane, raised the landing gear, and began a steady climb to the north, away from the Anacostia and Washington National traffic patterns.

Now they could breathe easier. The pilot's instrument panel had four nonelectrical instruments that operated by air pressure—the altimeter, airspeed indicator, rate-of-climb indicator, and a nonelectrical turn-and-bank indicator. These plus the gyro horizon and the other turn-and-bank indicator on the copilot's side gave them the essential instruments to keep the plane airborne in the fog—as long as the flashlight batteries held out.

Patterson glanced at his fuel gauges. They had frozen showing 525 gallons of gas when the electrical power went off. That would give the plane a little less than three hours of flying time.

The pilot continued his climb until he broke clear of the fog at about 3,500 feet. He began to fly a triangular pattern that the air controllers could easily see on their radarscopes. This is a standard emergency pattern that means: "I am lost and my radios are out. Send help."

On the ground, the controllers in Washington Approach Control saw pilot Patterson begin his triangular pattern. Radar centers throughout the surrounding area were alerted in case the lost plane took up a new course. All air traffic in the vicinity of Navy 40378 was rerouted to avoid any possibility of a collision. The watch supervisor called the Naval Air Station and put through an emergency request to launch another plane to guide Navy 40378 down to a safe landing. The controllers watched as Navy 40378 repeated the triangular pattern, patiently waiting for help.

There were four passengers in the main cabin of Navy 40378: Mr. and Mrs. Paul B. Fay, their four-year-old daughter, Sally, and a Navy aide, Commander William A. Golden. The next day was to be an important occasion for the Fay family. Mr. Fay was going to be sworn in by President John F. Kennedy as Undersecretary of the Navy. He had been given special permission to bring his wife and daughter down from New York in the Navy plane. Two older children, Katherine, 13, and Paul, 11, were in school and couldn't make the trip.

When the lights had gone out, Commander Golden, a Navy fighter pilot himself, had gone forward to see what had happened. The news he brought back was ominous.

"Mr. Secretary," he said, "we're in serious

trouble. We have less than three hours of gas and no way to land."

"What are our chances?" Mr. Fay asked.

"About one in a hundred."

Up front, pilot Patterson grew more and more uneasy as the minutes ticked away with no help arriving in response to the emergency pattern he was flying. By now a plane was being readied at Anacostia to guide him in, but Patterson, of course, had no way of knowing this. After more than half an hour of circling, he threw away the rule book and decided to gamble on a daring and unconventional plan.

Patterson and his copilot, Denton, were a rare breed of Navy pilot. They were among the last of the "flying chiefs"—noncommissioned chief petty officers who had gone through flight training in a special program in the 1940s. Once they got their wings they did nothing but fly—thousands of hours in all kinds of planes and in all kinds of weather. Between the two of them, Patterson and Denton probably had as much air time as any other two Navy pilots. And before the night was over they would put to use just about every trick they had ever learned.

With only two hours of fuel remaining now, Patterson knew that he could never reach any fog-free fields to the north, south, or west. The belt of fog along the coast was too extensive for that. He also knew that without the rest of his instruments he had no chance of locating and making an approach to any nearby fields.

So he headed east toward the Atlantic Ocean.

As he droned on through the night, his flight was tracked by radar controllers all along his route. Navy 40378 reached the shoreline near Delaware Bay and then, as the controllers watched in dismay, the plane disappeared from their radarscopes. They could do nothing now but send out search-and-rescue helicopters and ships to look for a plane that had crashed at sea—or so they thought.

But Patterson hadn't crashed. He had simply gotten too low for the radar to pick him up. When Patterson was sure that he was over open water, he slowly and cautiously began to descend through the fog. The sea had no tall buildings, TV towers, or hills to knock him out of the sky, and he knew that over the ocean there were sometimes clear patches in the fog.

Suddenly, out of the gloom, Patterson spotted lights below him. He eased the plane down to 500 feet and saw the running lights of a ship. The first part of his gamble had paid off. He had gotten beneath the fog safely. He turned back toward land until he and Denton could make out the faint, pale crests of surf breaking along the beach.

Could he make a safe, wheels-up landing on the sand? Hundreds of other planes had done it, but none, as far as Patterson knew, had been as big and heavy as the Convair transport. Still, the odds were better than landing in the sea.

"Get the passengers ready for a crash landing,"

he ordered. "We haven't got much time left."

Commander Golden and the flight attendant moved the Fay family to the front end of the passenger compartment and braced them with their backs to the forward wall. Though the little girl didn't understand what was happening, she began to cry.

Mr. Fay reached into his pocket and pulled out a piece of paper and a pencil, and in the dark wrote a note to his two absent children as best he could:

Darling Paul and Kath:
Your mother, father, and Sally are up on this plane without power, so I can't see to write this. It doesn't look too good, but we love you and if we must die now, we know that you will carry on. Your mother is very brave. We have said our prayers and our lives are in the hands of God. All our love.

Mom, Sal, and Dad

Suddenly the plane made a sharp turn. Patterson, flying in and out of fog at 300 feet, saw two parallel lines of lights glimmering feebly in the gloom. Could it possibly be a lighted airport runway? He wheeled the plane around in a steep bank and lowered his landing gear. The flight engineer was beaming the flashlight on the pilot's instrument panel with one aching arm and bracing himself with the other. Patterson came out of his turn and aimed for the faint row of lights. As they grew closer, they lined up in a familiar pattern. No doubt about it, they had found an airport! Patterson wasn't sure what field it was, but it looked awfully good. He touched down at the end of the runway and hit his brakes hard. But the runway was covered with water from a recent rain, and the tires had no traction. Even in good conditions, the runway was not designed for planes as large as the Convair. The plane reached the end of the strip, lurched over a mound of topsoil and settled slowly and gently into a few feet of water in a canal at the end of the field.

The crew and passengers scrambled out onto a wing. Within a few minutes help arrived from some

Mr. and Mrs. Paul Fay smile after their narrow escape.

homes near the field and everyone was carried safely ashore in rowboats. Navy 40378 had finally found a safe haven at Bader Field, a small airport outside Atlantic City, New Jersey. No matter how quiet things were, the manager of the field, a "good Samaritan" of the airways, always kept one runway lighted after he closed up for the night just in case someone was in trouble.

Paul Fay and his wife and daughter arrived in Washington one day late for the swearing-in ceremonies, and by that time the story of their narrow escape was in all the newspapers. Said President Kennedy as Mr. Fay was sworn in at the White House: "I never knew a fellow who went to such lengths to get publicity for a little ceremony like this!"

How "Wrong Way" Corrigan
Got His Name

Excitement was running high among the mechanics at the Ryan aircraft factory in San Diego, California.

"They say he's going to fly all the way from New York to Paris by himself."

"He looks more like a farmer to me. Do you think he knows how to fly?"

"We'll find out pretty soon. He's supposed to take up our new plane."

"Oh, no—it's not running right!"

The tall, lanky pilot arrived and took the plane up anyway, putting on a low-altitude stunt-flying exhibition at the field that surpassed anything that had ever been seen there before.

The mechanics and grease monkeys soon learned through the factory grapevine that the young pilot's name was Charles Lindbergh. He was really serious about a solo trans-Atlantic flight, and he wanted Ryan to build a special plane for the attempt.

At that moment one of the young men working in the factory began to dream that he, too, might someday fly across the Atlantic. It was a preposterous dream, as all good dreams should be, and the young man, Douglas Corrigan, did not dare reveal it to anyone. Who was he to be thinking such thoughts anyway? Just another kid from a broken home, unable to finish high school, just barely able to support himself and his younger brother by taking on jobs that no one else wanted.

The Ryan factory built *The Spirit of St. Louis*—the plane that Lindbergh ultimately flew to Paris—in just 60 days. Corrigan worked around the clock with the others in the factory to make sure it would get Lindbergh through. As *The Spirit of St. Louis* took shape, Corrigan learned all he could from the conversations around him about the performance needed for a trans-Atlantic trip, what equipment should be on board, what had to be left behind to save weight, what routes Lindbergh might fly.

Then the day came when Lindbergh flew to New York. The announcement of his arrival in Paris on May 21, 1927, was a moment of great jubilation for the hard-working crew at the Ryan plant. After that the excitement gradually died out. Corrigan put aside his own dream of a trans-Atlantic flight and returned to the difficult struggle to make a living.

Corrigan's dream seemed even less possible when the 1920s drew to a close and the country plunged into the Depression years of the 1930s. He drifted around the country looking for work in the aviation industry, which had been especially hard hit during those difficult years. But as time went by, Corrigan grew skillful enough to earn a mechanic's license, and by taking flying lessons instead of pay, he got a pilot's license, too.

In 1935 Corrigan returned to California and went to work once again at the Ryan aircraft factory. In the surroundings where it had been born, the dream came alive once more. He had managed to buy a plane of his own—a secondhand Curtiss Robin—from a down-and-out friend for 325 dollars. With its single engine and high wing, it looked very much like *The Spirit of St. Louis*, and it was just as old. In the evenings after work Corrigan began fitting out the Robin with extra gas tanks for long-distance flying.

By the mid-1930s, trans-Atlantic flights were no longer novel. Since Lindbergh, the ocean had been crossed many times by plane—in both directions— by a woman pilot, Amelia Earhart, flying solo in 1931; by a husband and wife team; by giant zeppelins from Germany; and, significantly, by two pilots from Eastern Airlines in a Lockheed Electra airliner. The world was on the verge of a commercial air service between the two continents, but Corrigan didn't care. Crossing the Atlantic was the one thing he really cared about. He said little but worked steadily at making his dream come true.

The old plane became a familiar sight at airports around Los Angeles as Corrigan worked on it and tested it. The other pilots jokingly called it "Corrigan's Clipper" and after a while government inspectors from the Department of Commerce began to take an interest in Corrigan's activities. So many U.S. pilots had crashed or disappeared while attempting flights over the Atlantic and Pacific that a flier was now required to have a special government license before taking off on a long transoceanic flight.

By August 1936 the Robin was ready for the trip as far as Corrigan was concerned. But a government inspector came out to the field, looked the plane over carefully, and shook his head.

"We'll license it for cross-country flights, but that's all," he said.

So Corrigan topped off his tanks with gas and headed east. When he got to New York, his request for a special license was turned down once more. "Put in some more tanks, get yourself an instrument flying rating, and maybe next time we'll let you go," he was told by the government inspectors. They

Douglas Corrigan, in grease-stained overalls, poses with his 1929 Curtiss Robin.

never really expected to see the shabby-looking young man or his old plane again.

It was getting late in the year for a trans-Atlantic flight anyway, so Corrigan flew back to California. To test himself and his plane, he worked out a 1,900-mile nonstop flight from New York to San Antonio, Texas, by way of Jacksonville, Florida. He reached San Antonio uneventfully the next morning, having covered a distance equal to that between Newfoundland and Ireland.

Back in California, he installed larger tanks in the Robin, brushed up on his instrument flying and once again applied for the license he needed. Again he was turned down. Amelia Earhart had just disappeared in the Pacific and the government would not license transoceanic flights of any kind.

So Corrigan flew east again. He had a map that showed two small fields in the northeast corner of Maine that might make good takeoff points for his flight. By landing at small, out-of-the-way airfields after dark, he made it across the continent without tipping off the government inspectors. But when he reached Maine he couldn't find his first-choice field.

He landed in a pasture and asked where the airport was.

"There ain't no airport here," a farmer told him. "They started to build one 'bout two years ago, but gave it up."

The next day he flew on to his second-choice

field, but found that heavy rains had cut a big gully across the middle of the field, making takeoffs in a heavily loaded plane impossible. Corrigan didn't want to risk being spotted at any larger fields, so he sneaked back to California the way he had come.

He had been in California only a few days when a new thought occurred to him. Why not land at New York's Floyd Bennett Field some evening after the officials have gone home and just fill up with gas and go? They couldn't hang a man for flying without a license. There would be no way to get weather reports—but that wouldn't be the first risk he had taken.

Corrigan overhauled his engine and then had an inspiration. "This plane has been the only little ray of sunshine in my life. So that's what I'll call her." He painted the name "Sunshine" on the nose of the Robin and headed east for the third time in 15 months. Ironically, he was forced down by rain six times before he got to New York. The trip took him eight days, and when he finally sneaked into an unused field on Long Island, he still had to wait two more days before the rain stopped.

By now it was the end of October and getting cold. The weather over the North Atlantic would be too chancy, so he returned to California again. This time he thought he would try to make it nonstop. He filled his tanks at Floyd Bennett Field to see what the reaction would be. No one tried to stop him, so he took off. For 29 hours he fought headwinds and bad weather. Finally, low fuel cut short his hopes near El Paso, Texas.

When he got to Los Angeles a few days later he was broke, hungry, and jobless. Two days after his arrival a government inspector spotted the plane and told Corrigan he could not fly it any more, not even around the field.

Corrigan soon got a job in another aircraft factory doing something for which he had plenty of experience—welding gas tanks—and *Sunshine* was tucked away in a hangar for the next six months. He overhauled the engine again and in the spring of 1938 asked innocently for permission to try a nonstop flight to New York and then return nonstop. *Sunshine* was in beautiful shape after its six-month rest, and Corrigan was obviously a capable pilot. So he was given permission to fly nonstop to New York. "If you get there nonstop, we'll certainly give you permission to fly back nonstop," the inspector told him.

Corrigan was elated. "The hard work's over—now all I have to do is make the flights!"

He put 100 gallons of gasoline in his plane and told his friends at the Los Angeles airport that he had to go to Texas. Then he flew down the coast to Long Beach and put in 145 additional gallons for "a trip to El Paso." That way no one at either airport knew he had enough gas to fly across the country. And if he didn't get to New York, neither the inspec-

Corrigan makes news by flying non-stop from Long Beach, California, to New York's Roosevelt Field in July, 1938.

tors nor anyone else would realize that the flight had been a failure.

The flight was a rough one but Corrigan made it nonstop, landing at Roosevelt Field, Long Island, with only four gallons of gas left. He spent a week getting *Sunshine* ready for the next flight. A few reporters were mildly interested in his nonstop coast-to-coast flight, but Howard Hughes was getting ready to start a record-breaking around-the-world flight and received most of the attention.

On Saturday, July 16, 1938, Corrigan packed up all his belongings (one pair of pants and one extra shirt), his lunch (two boxes of Fig Newtons and a candy bar), a quart bottle of water, and one map (of the United States). Then he flew over to Floyd Bennett Field to gas up and go. He told the hangar attendant that he wanted to leave by midnight.

A few minutes before midnight the airport manager called and told Corrigan that he would not be cleared for takeoff until morning. "By the way," he asked, "do you have a special license for this trip?"

"You bet I do. You can check it by calling the inspectors," said Corrigan. He had no license, of course, but hoped that it was too late at night to check with Washington. Besides, he had already demonstrated his ability to fly long distances by making *seven* coast-to-coast flights, paying every cent of the expenses from what he had earned doing odd jobs in the aviation industry. No government bureaucrat was going to stop him from realizing his dream at this point.

At 4 A.M. the airport manager arrived and helped Corrigan roll out his plane. The hangar attendant swung the prop, but didn't do it right. So Corrigan started the plane himself, then gave it a last-minute check with a flashlight while it was warming up. He thanked the airport manager and asked, "Which way should I take off?"

Corrigan checks his engine one last time before taking off for Ireland. He claimed he was flying back to California.

"Any direction you want," said the manager.

Twenty-six hours later Corrigan was over Ireland.

His dream was fulfilled, but he had some explaining to do. A pursuit plane came up and led him to a military airfield. An Irish army officer was there to meet him when he taxied in.

"My name's Corrigan. I left New York yesterday morning, headed for California, but I got mixed up in the clouds and turned the wrong way!"

"Yes, we know," said the officer with a twinkle in his eye. Corrigan's story didn't fool the Irish and it didn't fool the rest of the world. But he was a hero nonetheless. Any man with the courage to fly 2,000 miles "the wrong way" could hardly be a villain.

Said the head of the U.S. Bureau of Air Commerce, whose inspectors Corrigan had finally eluded: "It was a great day for the Irish. Because he succeeded so well, we must admire his courage—in the judgment of many, plain foolhardiness—but we earnestly hope that there will not follow in his wake the usual host of aspirants who will want to ride to glory by the same route."

When Corrigan returned to New York he was "rewarded" with one of the biggest tickertape parades of the year. His punishment—suspension of his

Corrigan poses for his surprised Irish hosts after landing at Baldonnel Aerodrome near Dublin on July 19, 1938.

pilot's license—expired the day before he arrived home by ocean liner.

Though Corrigan's flight has been all but forgotten, his fame lives on. To this day, people speak of pulling a "wrong-way Corrigan" when someone starts off in one direction and ends up going the other way.

What Happened to Them Later

The final chapter has not yet closed for many of the pilots whose exciting adventures are told in this book. But quite a few are gone now, and for those who flew in the perilous early days of aviation, a flying career was often tragically short.

Cal Rodgers, whose 84-day coast-to-coast odyssey is an epic of courage and persistence, was killed in a plane crash in 1912, just a few weeks after he finally reached the Pacific Ocean. While flying along the shore at Long Beach, California, not far from where he had triumphantly washed his wheels in the surf, he ran into a flock of sea gulls, lost control of his Wright biplane, and cartwheeled into the sea.

Channel flier Harriet Quimby's fame was short-lived, too. The same year she crossed the Channel she died in a bizarre accident while flying at an air meet in Boston. Coming in over Boston Harbor for a landing, her plane unaccountably flipped over while still several hundred feet up. Harriet Quimby fell out—pilots didn't wear seat belts in those days—and plunged to her death in the harbor.

Naval aviator John Rodgers, who sailed his disabled seaplane to Hawaii in 1925, died at the pinnacle of his career a year later in a landing accident on a routine flight from Washington, D.C., to Philadelphia. Andes conqueror Jean Mermoz also was lost at the height of his career. While making the first crossing of the South Atlantic in a radical new transoceanic airliner in December 1936, Mermoz was forced down in the sea by engine trouble and was never seen again.

After their flight to Spitsbergen in 1928, Hubert Wilkins and Carl Ben Eielson continued their work in the far North, but in different directions. In 1931 Wilkins commanded the first submarine voyage under the Arctic ice pack and took it to within 500 miles of the North Pole. Later in the 1930s he led several overland expeditions in the Arctic, then became an Arctic consultant for the U.S. government during World War II. He died quietly in retirement in Massachusetts in 1958. Eielson returned to Alaska after the Spitsbergen flight and became the most famous of the legendary Alaska "bush pilots." He gave his life trying to rescue the crew of an icebound freighter, disappearing in a storm somewhere over Siberia.

Australian pioneer Charles Kingsford-Smith died as he perhaps would have wished. He was last heard from over the Bay of Bengal on a long flight from England to Australia in his unending effort to establish air service between Australia and the rest of the world. P. G. Taylor, Smith's cool-nerved, oil-changing copilot on the New Zealand flight in 1935, continued on to a brilliant career. He became the first to cross the Indian Ocean and pioneered many other air routes in the South Pacific. Knighted by Queen Elizabeth in 1954, he lived in Australia until his death in 1967.

"Wrong Way" Corrigan's story had a truly happy ending. With the money he made from guest appearances after his mad escapade over the Atlantic in 1938, he bought an orange grove in California. He gradually retired from flying to tend his orange grove and is living there today—with his beloved *Sunshine* still with him and never out of sight for long.

The more recent pilots have fared well. Chuck Yeager was reassigned from test piloting after his wild ride in 1953 to the relative calm (to him, at least) of jet fighter squadrons, and is now an Air Force general. Marine Colonel Rankin also remained in jet fighters after his fall through the thunderstorm, flew a tour of combat duty in Vietnam, and retired recently. "Flying Chiefs" William Patterson and Martin Denton likewise continued in flying duty for the Navy after getting Navy Undersecretary Paul Fay and his family down safely in 1961. Both have since retired from the Navy.

Philip Ippolito, who landed on the George Washington Bridge when he was only 19, has remained an avid pilot. He amassed more than 6,000 hours of pilot time as a flight instructor and charter pilot and is now flying full-time with American Airlines.

Mrs. Joan Steinberger has flown in every Powder Puff Derby since she sacrificed her chance to win in 1969. She lives in California with her husband and two sons and continues to fly medical emergency supplies. She hasn't won a Derby yet. But she is still trying, and, anyway, for her winning isn't always the most important thing.

Index

Page numbers in italics refer to photographs.